PRIME MINISTER

PRIME MINISTER

The Conduct of Policy under
Harold Wilson and James Callaghan

Bernard Donoughue

JONATHAN CAPE
THIRTY-TWO BEDFORD SQUARE
LONDON

Dedicated in memory of Philip Williams,
teacher, scholar and friend,
with the wish that
Rachel, Kate, Stephen and Paul
will have his warmth, humour
and generosity of spirit

First published 1987
Copyright © 1987 by Bernard Donoughue

Jonathan Cape Ltd, 32 Bedford Square, London WC1B 3EL

British Library Cataloguing in Publication Data
Donoughue, Bernard
Prime Minister: the conduct of policy
under Harold Wilson and James Callaghan
1. Great Britain——Politics and government
——1974–1979
I. Title
354'.4107'2'09   DA592

ISBN 0–224–02450–7

Phototypeset by Falcon Graphic Art Ltd
Wallington, Surrey
Printed in Great Britain by
Ebenezer Baylis & Son Ltd
The Trinity Press, Worcester and London

Contents

Illustrations

Acknowledgments

The author would particularly like to thank The Lady Murray of Gravesend, Sir Douglas Wass, Sir John Hunt, David Piachaud, Gavyn Davies and Andrew Graham for their personal photographs. Other photographs are reproduced with the kind permission of: Les Wilson/Camera Press (no. 18); Central Office of Information (no. 17); Keith Hammet (no. 35); Monitor Press (no. 27); The *Observer*/Neil Libbert (no. 6) and David Newell Smith (no. 7); The Photo Source (nos 9, 10, 21 and 32); Popperfoto (no. 13); Press Association (nos 2, 8, 11, 15, 33 and 34); Syndication International (nos. 1, 3, 4, 5, 23, 28 and 29); *The Times* (nos 12 and 20); Topham Picture Library (no. 14).

Introduction

At No.10 Downing Street from 1974–9 I held the office of Senior Policy Adviser to the Prime Minister. I was the head of the new Downing Street Policy Unit, which contained some seven to ten experts whose job it was to brief the Prime Minister on the whole range of policy issues coming before him. This study does not attempt comprehensively and chronologically to cover everything that happened under the three Labour administrations which held office between 1974–9. It is concerned with the central issues which involved the Prime Minister. The minutiae of outer Whitehall and especially of Westminster are omitted, or are mentioned only in so far as they had an impact on Downing Street. *Prime Minister* therefore offers a selective view from the top. As such it forms the basis for an analysis of the nature of prime ministerial power and makes an attempt to assess the extent to which we experience 'prime ministerial' government in Britain.

In the first chapter I focus on the Prime Ministership itself – the Prime Minister at work, the power of that great office, and the central capability of Whitehall which serves the Premier. The next chapter is concerned with the February 1974 general election and the context in which Harold Wilson then came into power to head his third and fourth administrations. The following two chapters deal with the fields of economic policy, political economy and the interaction between the two. Chapter 3 examines counter-inflation and the Social Contract, and particularly the construction of the incomes policy of 1975–6. Chapter 4 covers the IMF episode of 1976, giving an inside story of what happened during that crisis. There follows a survey of other policy areas, including social policy, housing, health and Ireland. After describing the economic successes of 1976–8, I give an analysis of why Mr Callaghan did not call an election in

1978 and then a description of the disastrous 1978–9 Winter of Discontent, with some final conclusions.

Originally I had in mind to write a much larger, more detailed and comprehensive work on the 1974–9 Labour Government. That intention was based on the assumption that when I left Downing Street I would return to the more leisurely corridors of academia with the secretarial resources and above all the time to produce definitive textbooks. In the event, life in a City office from 7.30 am to 6.00 pm, often with four evenings a week in Parliament, has constrained that ambition (though satisfying others).

This work has therefore been written during short holidays, late evenings and occasional free weekends. Actually it is probably better for being briefer and more selective. It was certainly a relief to write without needing documentation or the dragging weight of footnotes. Apart from consulting contemporary newspapers for chronology and official government publications for economic statistics, for once I was writing about something I knew from first-hand observation and participation; that was a pleasure and a privilege. Consequently there is no bibliography, although the interested reader will benefit enormously from consulting the relevant writings of Bagehot and Richard Crossman on the British constitution, of John Macintosh on the British Cabinet, of Professors G.W. Jones and Anthony King on the office of Prime Minister, and of Joe Haines on the realities of life inside Harold Wilson's Downing Street.

I was greatly assisted both by the discipline imposed on me and the contributions from other participants in a term of seminars I delivered on this subject in 1983 at Nuffield College, Oxford, where I am proud to be an Associate Member of the Senior Commonroom. The Warden of Nuffield, Michael Brock, together with my old friend David Butler and my now sadly missed dear friend Philip Williams, gave enormous encouragement. If this book succeeds in combining the intellectual approach of a former university teacher of politics with the knowledge and insights derived from the privilege of having worked for five and a half years inside Downing Street, it will hopefully have justified some of their faith.

September 1986   B.D.

1

Prime Ministers and the British System of Central Government

To most British people Downing Street is a large black door guarded by a benign and decorative policeman. Occasionally the door opens briefly to let in or out a preoccupied Cabinet Minister or a waving Prime Minister with a coy entourage. More normally the door shuts in the small closed world of prime ministerial power.

I first entered that privileged world on the evening of 4 March 1974, having just come from Buckingham Palace with the new Prime Minister, Harold Wilson, and his four closest advisers. Cheering and booing crowds gathered along the pavements of Downing Street. Journalists and television crews jostled and cameras flashed. Once inside, however, the racket and circus of electioneering was not only shut out but seemingly totally erased. Silently lining the hallway and long corridor stretching from the front door to the Cabinet Room at the back of the house were the staff of No. 10. They seemed momentarily apprehensive but then broke into applause, led by the Principal Private Secretary, Robert Armstrong. The gesture was a little self-conscious, given that barely an hour earlier they had tearfully waved goodbye to the outgoing Prime Minister, Edward Heath. Yet it is a civilised convention, conveying the continuity of British politics and the tradition and mythology that British civil servants serve all their Prime Ministers with equal loyalty. Anyway, the applause broke the ice. Mr Wilson led us forward, shaking hands with his staff. I was encouraged to acknowledge a wink and a smile from a Private Secretary whom I had met socially. My main preoccupation, however, was to

1

secure a good office. In politics two of the most important ingredients of power are information and access. I needed a room which would be close enough to the Cabinet Room and to the Private Secretaries to know what was going on; and close enough to the Prime Minister to gain ready access to him at short notice. Earlier, while waiting at the Palace, I had discussed the geography of No. 10 with Joe Haines, Mr Wilson's experienced Press Secretary. He knew exactly the location he wanted for the Press Office and advised me to take a suite of rooms close to the Cabinet Room and near the stairway to the Prime Minister's study. We both broke off from the ceremony of introductions and speedily laid claims to our respective offices. With that main business executed, I relaxed and wandered through the corridors and rooms of that curiously silent house. Although it is in many ways just a large residence – in fact two seventeenth-century town houses connected back to back – I felt awed and humbled by the strong sense of history which attaches to it. I was lucky to be able to share the world of No. 10 for the next five years with two Prime Ministers. In what follows I will try to describe how the Prime Minister works and how that Downing Street world serves him or her.

It may be helpful to state what a Prime Minister does. Basically, five central roles are combined in the one person occupying No. 10 Downing Street. The first and primary role is governmental; as Chairman of the Cabinet the Prime Minister acts as head of the executive side of government (the other roles are more explicitly 'political', as will be described below). He is also the Minister who is ultimately in charge of the Civil Service; as supervisor of the executive machine he is concerned – sometimes nominally, sometimes actively – with the appointment of senior officials. He becomes involved, occasionally too closely, in the award of honours. Senior appointments in the Church are also advised on from No. 10 and a whole suite of beautiful rooms in that constricted building is devoted to this arcane process. (I initially tried to effect the removal of the Church from No. 10 in order to create room for other bodies more centrally involved in national affairs, but Robert Armstrong refused, saying that we never knew when the bishops might return to the centre of political debate. As was often the case, Robert was right.) Above all, the Prime Minister has a policy strategy role, being the only Minister with the authority to co-ordinate the policies of all other Cabinet Ministers. The ensuing descriptions of the 1975–6 crises over pay policy and over the International Monetary Fund (IMF) and the débâcle of the Winter of Discontent in 1979 illustrate the importance of this co-ordinating and strategic function. They also demonstrate that the Prime Minister's responsibilities as First Lord of the Treasury may be much more than nominal.

Three other roles carried out by the Prime Minister are political. As the leader of his party in the country, he frequently addresses party gatherings as well as (in the case of the Labour Party) attending fractious meetings of the party's National Executive. As the leader of the governing party in Parliament, he is required to take the lead in major debates, to face the ordeal of Question Time on Tuesdays and Thursdays, and to give leadership and encouragement to a motley band of back-benchers, many of whom believe that they could make a better success of his job and all of whom resent having been passed over for government office. He is also the national image-maker of both his government and his party, in which capacity he must demonstrate powers of leadership and present the public face which will attract the electorate at general elections, which are to a great extent fought on the basis of the perceived successes and failures of the Prime Minister. Finally, the Prime Minister is temporarily the elected head of the nation (the Monarch being the permanent Head of State) and as such is expected to represent the interests of the whole community.

These five basic prime ministerial roles – as head of the executive in Cabinet and in Whitehall, as leader of the party and of the Government in Parliament, as field-marshal and national image-maker in gladiatorial elections, and as the repository of some vaguely defined national interest – need the servicing and back-up which is reflected in the working sections of No. 10 Downing Street. The Private Office secretaries and the Policy Unit service the executive and policy roles conducted through Cabinet and Whitehall. The Political Office provides support for the national and local party role. The parliamentary role is aided by a mixture of the political office, the Private Secretary who is responsible for parliamentary affairs and the MP who serves as the Prime Minister's Parliamentary Secretary. The image-making role is provided on a day-to-day basis by the Press Office at No. 10, although all other sections also contribute to this latter function, positively or negatively. The Prime Minister's role as leader of the nation is also assisted by all sections of his office, although ultimately the interpretation and execution of this post lies in his hands alone.

The job of Prime Minister involves a dimension which is usually described as 'power', as well as merely being part of the machinery of government. The sources of that power are derived from a number of the Prime Minister's functions. He appoints (and dismisses) Ministers; he chairs the Cabinet and influences the agenda; he can issue instructions to the civil service; he leads the governing party; he has a wide spread of patronage; he has virtually automatic access to the media; he has usually (although not in Mr Callaghan's case) received the blessing and authority of a recent general election mandate; and, less tangibly but very importantly, he has inherited, however briefly, the impressive charisma of his mighty office. If all of these constituents are added together, the result is the special political compound which makes up prime ministerial power.

Most discussions of prime ministerial power are concerned with his or her positive capacity to influence and to execute policies. In fact, there are very severe limitations to that power. Indeed, for much of the five and a half years during which I served in Downing Street, I was more aware of the constraints on, than the massive impact of, prime ministerial power. Personal constraints are unavoidable: the limitation of time and energy, of just how much one man or woman can do. There are also what may be called the permanent 'structural' constraints: the constant need in a collective system of government to secure the support of Cabinet colleagues and of the party. Equally important, in the context of influencing policies, are the prior constraints – the basic fact that most policies start elsewhere. Policies are not generally born in No. 10; it is more usual for them to be finalised there. Many begin with party programmes, party conferences and party manifestos. (The recent efforts of the Labour left wing to make previous policy promises voted for at party conferences totally binding on any future Labour governments are therefore a diminution of prime ministerial power, although of course if any of the leading protagonists of this view ever became Prime Minister he or she would almost certainly undergo a dramatic conversion to more traditional ideas about the need to locate policy-making power in Downing Street.) Other policies are generated in the relevant Whitehall ministry; every department has its inherited history of views towards a particular policy area, regardless of the party in power or Minister in office. However, individual Ministers do themselves have policy preferences and these too will influence policies (often via a curious process of debate with their own officials, described with devastating accuracy in the television series 'Yes Minister'). Outside pressure groups also have a major influence in a corporate state such as ours. The TUC had enormous, perhaps excessive, influence on the Labour governments described in this book. Equal pressures are exercised on Conservative governments, although the successful groups differ – being comprised of landowners, farmers, the military, merchant bankers and the old professions. (One of Mrs Thatcher's more attractive features, although perhaps her ultimate weakness within her party, was that for a long time she tried to resist these traditional Tory vested interests in the hope of establishing a more efficient and meritocratic society in Britain.)

Whitehall is also a constraint in itself. The machine can actually influence and limit policies while nominally going through the merely administrative function of processing. This phenomenon was evident in the formulation of pay policy in 1975. The Cabinet Office in particular may constrain policy-making (or accelerate it) because it establishes the agenda for policy discussion and selects and co-ordinates the participating departments, thus shaping the structure, balance and timetable of policy debate. Cabinet Committees discuss and amend policy proposals, and of course on major issues the Cabinet itself finally makes the decision. Therefore there is a whole panoply of constraints built into the policy-making process. Each of those is a potential, and often a real, limitation upon the Prime

Minister's nominally great power to influence policy.

Within this structure it is not often easy for a Prime Minister to see how he or she can personally intervene to initiate, amend or reject policies. Every policy area has a sponsoring department and a natural procedure for discussion, approval and implementation. Indeed, it is not always clear whether a Prime Minister should do any personal policy-making; there have been Prime Ministers who in fact avoided this. It is easy and tempting to allow the policy-making process to follow its own well-worn Whitehall course.

The Prime Minister's basic policy role, when he or she chooses to exercise it, in the face of all the constraints, is not related to a specific policy area, but is rather to sustain and co-ordinate the coherence of government policy-making as a whole. In addition, frequently his or her contribution is to introduce a dimension which is wider than departmental. It may often be seen as a national dimension, something called the national interest, difficult though that may be to define. A Prime Minister may feel that a department is, understandably, taking too narrow a departmental view, or, even more understandably, that a departmental Minister is taking a view that is too politically partisan. The Prime Minister may then intervene to interpolate a wider governmental or national perspective. Conversely, of course, Ministers sometimes 'go native' in their departments and the Prime Minister may feel compelled to introduce a degree of party political realism into that Minister's proposals. Such, on my observation, were the kinds of wider dimensions and horizons most regularly introduced by a Prime Minister into the policy-making process, whether from the Cabinet chair, directly to a Minister in conversation, or by a prime ministerial minute.

However, it is open to a Prime Minister to intervene with personal initiatives in specific areas of micro-policy. The ensuing descriptions of the crises on pay and the IMF, on the planning to exploit North Sea oil, and the discussions of the Winter of Discontent show this. Mr Wilson took other initiatives over Ireland, the sale of council houses, commodities pricing and the film industry, as did Mr Callaghan in the fields of education, hospitals, personal tax reform, nuclear policy and aircraft purchasing policy. In each case it involved intervention in the normal Whitehall processes and often upset the respective departmental Ministers and officials who believe that Prime Ministers should not trespass on their policy cabbage patches (the Department of Education's reaction to Mr Callaghan's 1976 Ruskin speech was the worst example of this, whereas the Treasury, being of a much higher calibre, was often commendably relaxed about much more disruptive economic interventions from Downing Street). Although the general public may view the Prime Minister as having supreme power in government, Whitehall certainly assumes and prefers that he or she (as Mrs Thatcher presumably learned) does not exercise it.

The extent to which a Prime Minister intervenes in the policy process, and whether he can intervene effectively and so make an impact on policy, depends on numerous factors. A long list of possible variables could be constructed. However, there are only four major factors which normally determine whether or not a Prime Minister is likely to intervene and then whether he intervenes successfully. Firstly, there is the personal factor – the temperament, background and personal style of the Prime Minister of the day. Secondly, there is the political factor – the Prime Minister's power and standing in relation to fellow Cabinet Ministers. Then there is the administrative factor – the scale and competence of the advisory services available to the Prime Minister in Downing Street. The last major variable is the opportunity of events, as it is the big issues, such as incomes policy, the IMF, the Falkland Islands invasion, which enable a Prime Minister to take the limelight on the policy stage. It may be helpful to look at these factors in the context of Prime Ministers Wilson and Callaghan.

Dealing first with the last of these four major factors, the nature and pressure of events arising within the main policy fields is to some degree unquantifiable and unforecastable. To a great extent economic events, for example, are threatening or, conversely, manageable according to how the Government itself sees or assesses them. There is, however, a perceptible objective difference between, on the one hand, the routine management of existing economic policies and, on the other, a crisis which may be threatening the whole economic strategy of the Govern-

ment. Routine matters will normally be conducted internally by
the Treasury, with the Chancellor only periodically reporting to
Cabinet and to Parliament. Routine economic policy does not
usually come before the Prime Minister in any systematic or
meaningful way. Crises, however, such as those described in this
book concerning inflation, pay policy, public expenditure, the
currency, the IMF, and the Winter of Discontent, require the
active involvement of Cabinet and provide the Prime Minister
with an opportunity to intervene. In these aforementioned crises
the Government's whole economic strategy was in jeopardy (and
in some cases damaged). The Government's commitments to its
own party election manifesto were in question and were in some
cases abandoned. Cabinet Ministers found their departmental
programmes to be in danger. The new policy remedies which
were proposed required full Cabinet support against inevitable
political unpopularity. The Chancellor in particular wanted the
approval of his Prime Minister and colleagues in order to spread
the responsibility collectively. He also needed the Prime Minister to lead and deliver the support of other Ministers. The
Treasury is usually very isolated in Cabinet, having only two
ministerial members (and only one until 1977 when the Financial Secretary, Joel Barnett, was promoted), and it always
needed the support of at least a dozen other Cabinet Ministers.
Many of these were from spending departments which would
suffer from the impact of tough economic measures. Some
colleagues may even have had their eyes on the Chancellor's job,
thus diminishing their enthusiasm to offer him assistance in his
hour of need. Therefore, in these crises, the Chancellor needed
his Prime Minister to rally such colleagues behind him and this
in turn gave the Prime Minister an enhanced opportunity to
intervene. It is in this kind of situation that the Prime Minister –
provided that he has the personal interest, inclination and
will, the authority over his colleagues and the relevant ideas
and economic arguments – can decisively influence economic
policy.

The personal factor in prime ministerial government is
obviously a psychological minefield on which political scientists
must tread with care. Certainly, to succeed Prime Ministers
need three basic characteristics: strong ambition, unusual luck

and, above all, remarkable physical stamina. Without these elements it is unlikely that a politician will become Prime Minister. Several other positive traits will be helpful to a Prime Minister, but without these basic qualities he or she probably will not get to Downing Street. Given the basic requirements, a whole range of personalities may become Prime Minister in Britain and indeed have done so. This is not least because the individuals concerned (with the obvious exception of Churchill in the war) are usually selected primarily not on the basis of their being a suitable Prime Minister but as a party leader capable of holding the party together and winning an election.

In terms of career backgrounds both Harold Wilson and James Callaghan had remarkably long experience in national politics (certainly much more than the average American President who often reaches Washington from a distant State riding on a cloud of media hype rather than on substantial national experience). Each of them had been in Parliament since 1945 and each served in Attlee's 1945–51 Government (Wilson in the Cabinet, Callaghan in a more junior capacity). Admittedly Harold Wilson had run only one Whitehall department (Trade) before becoming Prime Minister and in that sense he could be described as inexperienced in 1964. However, by the time I joined him in 1974 he had already been Prime Minister for nearly six years covering two administrations in the 1960s and he exuded Whitehall know-how. By 1976, when he took over No. 10, Mr Callaghan had almost unprecedented governmental experience. He had held the three great traditional offices of State, the Treasury, the Home Office and the Foreign Office, something which no other twentieth-century Prime Minister had achieved. He had also served as a Minister in five departments in Whitehall and knew the machinery inside out. Perhaps partly because of his experience in Whitehall, Mr Callaghan was more willing than Harold Wilson to intervene in the affairs of other departments. In particular, he showed absolutely no deference towards the Treasury. As a former Chancellor, he was very supportive of Denis Healey, knowing what it was like to be alone in the trenches with flak coming from every direction; but equally he was not intimidated by the Treasury mystique. By contrast, Harold Wilson seemed over-respectful towards the

Treasury, perhaps even a little frightened, and kept himself more at arm's length from his Chancellor.

In terms of personality the two men were strikingly dissimilar: each impressive but in quite different ways. Wilson was clever, subtle, pleasant to be with, very easy-going, and he had absolutely no side at all. He was soft in manner and certainly disliked confrontation, often delegating when it was necessary to be disagreeable to people. Mr Callaghan, by contrast, was tough, determined, often authoritarian in style and usually willing to face problems head on, which Harold Wilson was reluctant to do. It was said that in his early days James Callaghan was less tough and sometimes a bit blustering, but by the time of my acquaintance he had hardened and his civil servants were in awe of him. Shirley Williams, who had known him for a long time, once said to me: 'You know, Jim has toughened over time from the outside in.' Certainly it was not enjoyable to be on the wrong side of him. With me, however, he was always courteous, reliable, interested and very satisfying to work for. In style and approach he was potentially one of the finest Prime Ministers of twentiety-century Britain, although the lack of a parliamentary majority and the misfortune of the events that dogged him limited the fulfilment of that potential.

The two men had very different origins in life which were greatly in evidence. Harold Wilson never seemed to lose the traces of his early career as a grammar-school achiever, Oxford don and high-flying civil servant. He liked to display his intellectual skill and was ever respectful of the sleek civil service machine. Having served early on in the Cabinet Office secretariat, his respect for the hierarchy, with the Cabinet Secretary sitting at the peak, was established for life.

On the other hand, James Callaghan was raised in straitened circumstances by his widowed mother, and was forced to leave school at the age of fourteen. He was therefore the only British Prime Minister born in the twentieth century not to have attended university. This mattered only because he apparently felt it did. He had an initial suspicion of overtly 'clever' people and seemed at times to doubt his own cleverness. In fact he had a most formidable, if not obviously refined, intellect, which in politics was to his advantage, backed as it was by a remarkably wide experience of life. Anyone who questioned James Callaghan's mental capacity needed only a few minutes' exposure to remove those doubts. On one occasion early in his Premiership he sent for the brilliant young economic adviser in the Policy Unit, Gavyn Davies. Gavyn returned an hour later, white and limp from the grilling on economics which had taken place, and pronounced it more testing than anything during his time at Oxford. I frequently felt the same. Mr Callaghan had a devastating capacity for asking the simple central question which did not allow for anything other than the simple central answer, which so often one did not quite have. One was given little opportunity to avoid the central question through conventional intellectual discussion of all the conundra and penumbra, pursuing intricate pathways and describing the many sides of an issue. His was an astute intelligence, except when he grew physically exhausted, as happened during the 1978–9 Winter of Discontent, and then his mind slowed with his body. He was also, by the 1970s, more interested in actual policies than was Harold Wilson, who had expended enormous energy and curiosity on a wide range of policy fields in the 1960s but by 1974 suffered from a sense of *déjà vu*. Mr Wilson once said to me: 'I have been round this racetrack so often that I cannot generate any more enthusiasm for jumping any more hurdles.' This was perhaps the single most important reason why in 1976, with commendable self-awareness, he resigned at the age of sixty. Mr Callaghan had by then abandoned hope of becoming Prime Minister in the 1970s. Although several years older than his predecessor, he came to the job unexpectedly and therefore with a fresh interest. This was one more factor, together with his *dirigiste* temperament and wider departmental experience, which probably made him by the 1970s the more inclined of the two to intervene in policy matters.

Both men were capable of such prodigious work that it was humiliating for me as a much younger person to see these elderly gentlemen working between fourteen to sixteen hours a day, often seven days a week and up to fifty weeks a year. The adrenalin of high office makes light of the years. Wilson clearly had the highest potential work rate and when Prime Minister during the 1960s had exploited it to the full, working round the clock without sleep, rather like a modern business tycoon. During his 1974–6 administrations he performed in this way more rarely, perhaps because he was less interested and no longer excited by being Prime Minister. He also suffered bouts of poor health, with heart flutters in 1975, and towards the end of his Premiership he slackened perceptibly. However, he was still occasionally capable of drawing on his reserves, and when any crisis arose he smartly slipped into overdrive. Mr Callaghan did not possess such stamina as his predecessor. He paced himself carefully and needed regular hours of sleep, so he would usually snatch a nap in the afternoon and often again in the evening.

Their styles of working were also quite different. Mr Callaghan liked to take one subject – aerospace, nuclear power, the European monetary system – and concentrate on that for weeks at a time. He did not welcome being sidetracked on any other policy subject. If I sent him a memo on social policy or child benefits or training production engineers while he was otherwise occupied, it would remain at the bottom of his box or else would disappear, unread, into an inside pocket or under the bed, to be returned weeks later when out of date. By contrast, Harold Wilson loved jumping from topic to topic. He was a natural grasshopper in the policy meadows.

Harold also liked verbal advice and a lot of gossip. He loved chatting. He would emerge from the heavy dramas of the Cabinet room and grab me, saying, 'Get Joe [Haines], get Albert [Murray], come upstairs to the study.' Once there, one moment we would be discussing international monetary policy, and the next the football disasters of Millwall FC (for which team Albert Murray, Wilson's lovable aide, had a lifelong and masochistic addiction) or the alleged affaires of various Ministers, especially at Defence, where the security aspect added a delicious piquancy. Working with Wilson was exciting, enjoyable, superficial and even chaotic. Mr Callaghan was much more formal in his method. He preferred to receive his briefing on paper and he liked it to be presented at an appropriate time in relation to a specific item on the Cabinet agenda, preferably sufficiently in advance to allow time for prior discussion which would ideally take place at a previously arranged meeting. James Callaghan did not appreciate advisers just dropping in, whereas with Harold we would simply knock and walk into the study saying, 'I've just had a thought on how we might make progress on child benefits,' whereupon he would look up from whatever he was reading and say, 'That's interesting, sit down and have a drink' (characteristically he always himself opened the beer bottles and poured drinks for his personal aides, rather than vice versa, or summoning the messengers always loitering outside the door to do it for him). Mr Callaghan would respond with equal interest, but was more likely to say, 'Good, can you put it down on paper and when I've read it we will have a meeting.' He did not like things to be sprung on him or to be rushed, preferring always to be well prepared. Then he was most impressive in his judgment and his decision-making.

Both men could be effective in their policy roles and knew how to work the Whitehall machine in order to influence government. They knew whom to send for, which instructions and requests should go out, which committees should be summoned and who should be appointed to them. They each had an uncanny sense of timing, of when was the right time to act on a policy and when it was more sensible to let matters lie. In sum, these were the kinds of personal factors – temperament, ability, career background, working style and approach – that influence a Prime Minister's potential effectiveness in terms of policy-making and which Prime Ministers Wilson and Callaghan both possessed.

The third factor which shapes the potential influence of a Prime Minister is his or her political standing, especially in relation to Cabinet colleagues. This is basically a question of authority. On economic policies it concerns the Prime Minister's authority *vis-à-vis* that of the Chancellor of the Exchequer. All Prime Ministers have a degree of authority independent of personal stature. Some authority is intrinsic to the position of Prime Minister: it comes naturally and automatically with the office. It was very striking to observe how, from the moment Mr Callaghan became Prime Minister, other politicians who had been friends and life-long colleagues began to behave differently towards him. There is a charisma attached to the occupancy of No. 10.

This is of course helpfully supplemented by the Prime Minister's unique power of 'hiring and firing' – the fact that in the end he can rid himself of Ministers who do not respect his authority. However, that capacity is not absolute, and is far more limited than is often realised. It is probably at its maximum when the Prime Minister, having just been selected by his party or voted in by the electorate, is forming a new administration. At that stage all Ministers have tendered their resignations and it is a question of appointments rather than sackings. Hence Mr Callaghan was able to drop two senior party figures, Mrs Barbara Castle and Mr William Ross, when forming his Cabinet in April 1976. At any other time it would have been difficult to sack them – especially Mrs Castle – without there being a fuss in the party. As it was, the attention was diluted over the wide changes in the Government and the publicity for the younger politicians being brought into the Cabinet. However, even when forming or reshuffling an administration, the 'hiring' power of the Prime Minister is limited because up to two-thirds of the appointments to Cabinet are pre-empted in the sense that some senior politicians, being barons in their party with a personal political following, cannot prudently be excluded by a Prime Minister when forming the Cabinet. Equally there are Ministers, usually again with strong party support, whom a Prime Minister finds it difficult to fire once the Cabinet is formed. Tony Benn was an obvious example during 1974–9, although Mr Callaghan believed that he could have sacked Benn without too much risk after an election victory when the Prime Minister would have benefited from the extra legitimacy of the electorate's mandate (not that Benn's dismissal would have been part of the Labour election manifesto, effective and electorally attractive though that might have been). Other Labour Ministers were also relatively immune. Wilson could not easily have dismissed James Callaghan in 1974–6; and neither Prime Minister would have found it easy to drop Denis Healey, although the possibility was considered in late 1976. So there are limitations to the hiring and firing power of Prime Ministers; but within those limitations it is still a factor encouraging the obedience of colleagues and thus reinforcing the authority of the man at the top.

Perceived political ability naturally strengthens a Prime Minister. By this I do not mean academic intellect. But as a party leader it is very important to be able to convince party conferences and equally important as a parliamentary performer to be able to impress the House of Commons. Both Mr Wilson and Mr Callaghan had that kind of standing and authority with their colleagues. Wilson's authority was uniquely founded on having won four out of the five general elections he had fought as party leader; Mr Callaghan lacked that legitimacy and was conscious of it as a weakness. Yet the latter dominated his Cabinet colleagues more than his predecessor during the 1970s. Mr Wilson was apparently more assertive a decade earlier. By 1974 his colleagues were more difficult to dominate. The Wilson administration of 1974–6 was probably, in terms of individual qualities and collective experience, the outstanding Cabinet of this century. James Callaghan, Roy Jenkins, Denis Healey, Barbara Castle, Tony Crosland, Harold Lever, not to mention Wilson himself, constituted a remarkably impressive team. They had such experience, intellectual calibre, seniority and weight in various sections of the party that it was not easy for any Prime Minister to dominate them. (It was in this respect easier for Mr Callaghan, as by 1977 only two of those veterans remained under him, younger politicians having moved in.) Probably Mr Wilson could have dominated his colleagues a little more in 1974–6 had he so chosen, but he was anxious not to repeat the 'presidential' experience of 1964. He told me in Liverpool on the eve of the February 1974 election that if elected back to Downing Street he proposed to adopt a lower profile – using his favourite football metaphors he said that this time he would 'play as a sweeper in defence, not a striker in attack'. He now had very experienced colleagues and he proposed to let them run their own sides of government; he would be 'a first among equals'. Thus it was that Wilson chaired the Cabinet rather than leading and dominating it. While he was feeling his way into the job Mr Callaghan was content merely to act as chairman, but after his success in the IMF crisis, which gave him greater authority, he dominated his colleagues very perceptibly. However, in terms of the capacity and political authority to influence policy when they chose, both Mr Wilson and Mr Callaghan were strongly positioned, as the events of 1975–6 demonstrated.

The final broad area which is important in determining the degree of the Prime Minister's influence on policy concerns the kind of advice which he receives, the expertise that is at his disposal, providing facts and figures and shaping arguments. This matters because the exercise of government is not a question of the Prime Minister simply issuing instructions. The conduct of British government involves a process of continual inter-departmental debate which frequently turns into intense and protracted trench warfare. Protagonists in these policy battles need a good supply of the ammunition of facts, figures and arguments. This is particularly true in battles with the Treasury, which is well armed with economists and statisticians prepared to provide the numerical arguments for any policy position. Unless the Prime Minister is able to argue with the Treasury using his own well-researched statistics, thus being able to point out that the Treasury case can be seen in a different light and that alternative policies can be supported statistically, he usually will not win. The Prime Minister not only has to deal with the Treasury but also with the various other Whitehall departments which themselves have thousands of troops servicing their current policy positions. A Prime Minister who inclines to take a different view is therefore inevitably under-powered. The British Prime Minister does not have a separate, permanent department of his own, unlike the American and French Presidents or the German Chancellor. To some extent the modest servicing of the British Prime Minister compared to that of his international counterparts simply reflects a lack of space. No. 10 Downing Street is a relatively small building composed of two back-to-back town houses. Its five floors contain various offices, four reception rooms, the Cabinet room, the Prime Minister's study and flat, and some bedrooms under the roof. In total there is space for a little over a hundred working people. The majority of these are secretaries, messengers and police officers. The number of people in senior advisory positions is inevitably limited, and there are no more than a dozen in all, with a similar quota of junior advisers.

The advisory staff are nearly all divided into four functional groups which service the Prime Minister's main roles described earlier in this chapter (Cabinet, party, parliamentary, media). The respective offices servicing these prime ministerial roles in Downing Street are: (i) the Private Office secretaries who are temporarily loaned to No. 10 by other Whitehall departments and who conduct the Prime Minister's official relations with Whitehall, Parliament and the public in his capacity as executive head of government; (ii) the Press Office, which handles the Prime Minister's relations with the media; (iii) the Political Office, which conducts the Prime Minister's affairs in his capacity as a Member of Parliament and as leader of a political party; and (iv) the Policy Unit which advises the Prime Minister on all areas of government policy.

The staff of the Private Office are always permanent civil servants, whereas those of the Political Office are always temporary outsiders. The Press Office has regular civil service information officers but it may be led either by an outsider, as with Harold Wilson bringing in Joe Haines, or a regular civil servant, as with Tom McCaffrey working for James Callaghan or Bernard Ingham for Mrs Thatcher. The Policy Unit which I ran between 1974–9 was composed entirely of temporary recruits from the outside world, although under Mrs Thatcher there has been some colonisation by the regular civil service.

The Prime Minister's Private Office is the single most important section of the administrative support services in No. 10. It is the communications centre of Downing Street, and is in regular contact with all the ministerial private offices. Virtually all official communications to or from the Prime Minister, written or verbal, are channelled through the Private Office. The Private Secretaries sift through the flow of papers and decide – based upon their experience of central government and upon their knowledge of a particular Prime Minister's interests and priorities – which to put before him urgently, which to delay, and which not to bother him with but to answer themselves. They fill the Prime Minister's red boxes for his nightly or his weekend reading. The Senior Secretaries will periodically sit with him in the study or in the flat discussing how to respond on certain issues. Usually a close bond of trust builds up between the Prime Minister and his Private Office, which organises the whole routine of his governmental working day. Few people, inside or outside government, enjoy such a devoted and such an efficient service. The danger is that Prime Ministers become entranced by and dependent on the support, which gives the Private Secretaries great potential power to influence. After leaving Downing Street most Prime Ministers feel deprived and may find it difficult to adjust once more to organising their own political lives.

The Private Secretaries occupy two high, crowded rooms next to the Cabinet room. The Principal Private Secretary sits in the smaller room of the two with his desk beside the large double doors guarding the side entrance into the Cabinet room. When we arrived in office in March 1974 the occupant of this powerful seat and the boss of the Downing Street administration machine was Robert Armstrong. A man of formidable intellect and authoritative bearing, he appeared to me quite daunting in our opening discussions on the role of the Policy Unit. He was undoubtedly concerned that the internal lines of communication to the Prime Minister in Downing Street should not be confused or his own status diminished. However, we rapidly established not only an excellent working relationship but also a personal friendship of mutual respect which has survived many changes of circumstances. He is a warm, complex and very sensitive man and comes professionally from the best civil service tradition of integrity and public duty. He was a Rolls Royce in Whitehall. His successor, Kenneth Stowe, was an easier and simpler man, entirely without side. He gave the Policy Unit every possible assistance and we worked closely and comfortably together. His great virtues were his calmness, his openness and his directness. Mr Callaghan thought the world of him and I could quite see why. He was a marvellous team member.

With the Principal Private Secretary sits the Foreign Affairs Private Secretary, usually a Foreign Office official who is expected to rise high in the ranks of the Diplomatic Service. In my time the three occupants of the post were Lord Bridges (son of a former Head of the Civil Service and later to be Ambassador to Rome), Bryan Cartledge (subsequently a predictably hawkish Ambassador to Moscow) and Patrick Wright, a marvellously amusing colleague who deservedly became head of the Diplomatic Service. These Foreign Service Secretaries all seemed a little set apart from the rest of us in No. 10. Perhaps it was simply because they were the only ones who were not members of the Home Civil Service. But it seemed to be more than that. Somehow they never ceased to be the Foreign Office representatives to the Prime Minister. The other Private Secretaries were unreservedly the Prime Minister's men.

The larger room is occupied by a group of younger Private Secretaries, each with a distinct specialisation. One, usually from the Treasury, concentrates on economic matters. While I was there a second domestic post was established to cover the rest of social policy. One secretary dealt with parliamentary affairs, specialising in predicting the wicked intentions behind the most innocent looking Commons questions. The Prime Minister's daily diary also required the full-time attention of a secretary (although under Mrs Thatcher this job was for a time carried out by a personal staff member and not by a regular civil servant). In practice any one of these secretaries might cover the field of an absentee and one of them always had to be available at the weekend. Finally, squeezed in one corner was a duty clerk who handled the multitude of routine office tasks and was on duty to take telephone calls and process any business which arose throughout the night.

The administrative quality of these young Private Secretaries was in my time extremely high. They were selected from the cream of their departments and with the help of their Downing Street experience were expected to rise to the top positions in the civil service. The three secretaries from the Treasury with whom I worked – Robin Butler, Nigel Wicks and Tim Lankester – were very impressive. Indeed, Robin Butler was the most outstanding civil servant with whom I ever had to deal, at any level. It was very important to the success of the Policy Unit that we should get on well with the Private Secretaries, especially those covering the economic field. They were a vital source of information for us. It was also helpful if their advice to the Prime Minister did not entirely conflict with ours. A Prime Minister is more likely to be impressed by a united No. 10 view. For this reason we worked very closely with the Private Secretaries and during some of the most stressful crises their support was absolutely essential.

The Policy Unit was the newest part of the Downing Street machine. Previous Prime Ministers had employed individual advisers. However, until Harold Wilson created the Policy Unit in 1974 there was no systematic policy analysis separate from the regular civil service machine and working solely for the Prime Minister. These are the three characteristics which distinguished the Policy Unit from what had existed before: it was systematic, it was separate from the Whitehall machine and it was solely working to the Prime Minister. This strengthening of the supportive mechanisms serving the Prime Minister has proved an important reform among the several contributions which Harold Wilson made to the effectiveness of British central government. It is significant that not only did James Callaghan retain the Policy Unit, but his Tory successor, Margaret Thatcher, continued and strengthened it.

Harold Wilson described the proposed Policy Unit as his 'eyes and ears' when asking me to create it in March 1974. I worked frantically during the early weeks interviewing and recruiting members. Our target was to have six to eight policy specialists together with a couple of research assistants. The recruitment was not always an easy procedure as candidates had little idea of how the new institution would work and some had observed the unhappy treatment of outside advisers previously admitted to Whitehall. Nor could they be offered much security. Special advisers are temporary civil servants and their appointments terminate automatically when their Minister leaves office – hence I received letters of dismissal in advance of the general elections of October 1974 and May 1979, and on 16 March when Harold Wilson announced his resignation. At first we were offered no redundancy terms but I subsequently negotiated some compensation for special advisers related to their years of service. However, in the spring of 1974, with another election expected soon, it was not possible to offer much security of tenure. Fortunately people of the highest ability are rarely motivated by a strong desire for security, and I was able to recruit a group of distinguished policy experts who worked in our three cramped rooms situated up the corridor from the

Cabinet room and the Private Offices and directly opposite the locked green baize door to the Cabinet Office – through which I could see from my desk Sir John Hunt, the Cabinet Secretary, frequently bustle, clutching his precious key. By the summer I was assisted by Andrew Graham, Fellow in Economics from Balliol College, Oxford; Gavyn Davies, a young economist also from Balliol; David Piachaud, a lecturer in social policy from the London School of Economics; Catherine Carmichael, lecturer in social administration at the University of Glasgow; Richard Graham, Manager of Domestic Trunks Services with British Airways; and Richard Kirwan, a housing economist from the Centre for Environmental Studies. They were later joined by Richard Smethurst and David Gowland, economists from Oxford and York Universities respectively, by Jim Corr from the World Bank and by Elizabeth Arnott from Transport House's social policy research staff. Often assisted by Mr Wilson's outstanding Press Secretary, Joe Haines, they constituted an intellectual power house with wide policy expertise and strong political awareness. Whipped into line by my personal assistant, Brenda Haddau, a brilliant young civil service administrative assistant, they made a formidable team without which I could have achieved very little.

The press release on the new Policy Unit issued from Downing Street stated that the Unit would 'assist in the development of the whole range of policies contained in the Government's programme, especially those arising in the short and medium term'. This was an attempt to distinguish it from the Central Policy Review Staff (CPRS), based in the Cabinet Office which was more, although not exclusively, orientated to longer-term policy horizons. Members of the Unit were specifically enjoined to maintain regular liaison with the CPRS, with other special advisers working for individual departmental Ministers, with the chairmen of policy committees of the parliamentary Labour party and with policy specialists in party headquarters. An internal memorandum to Unit members, drafted by myself and cleared by Mr Wilson, described the Unit's functions in detail: 'The Unit must ensure that the Prime Minister is aware of what is coming up from departments to Cabinet. It must scrutinise papers, contact departments, know the background to policy decisions, disputes and compromises, and act as an early warning system. The Unit may feed into the system ideas on policy which are not currently covered, or are inadequately covered ... The Unit should feed in "minority reforms" which departments may overlook, or which fall between departmental boundaries, or which are the subject of worthy but unsuccessful Private Members Bills. This is especially the case with issues which concern ordinary people (and of which Whitehall may be unaware).' The political dimension in its work was underlined: 'The Prime Minister has assumed responsibility as custodian of the Labour manifesto. The Unit must assist in that role, making sure that the manifesto is not contravened, nor retreated from, without proper discussion and advance warning ... Throughout its policy work the Unit will clearly be aware of the political dimension in Government. It must maintain good relations with the party organisation. The individual Ministries must not become isolated from the Government as a whole and lapse into traditional "departmental views".'

My next most important task after recruiting its members was to negotiate the Unit's working arrangements within Whitehall – and above all its rights to access to the decision-making process based on the jungle of committees. Without access one is impotent in Whitehall. I had prolonged and strenuous talks with the then Cabinet Secretary, Sir John Hunt. His concern, quite properly, was that the Unit advisers should not replace the normal Private Office channels of communication between No. 10 and Ministers on official business, which I accepted. In return he readily conceded that, as departmental Ministers did not have matching special advisory *cabinets*, the Unit would have to make direct links with officials. We were therefore authorised to be in immediate contact with other departments in order to discover 'official thinking on departmental policies'. Most important were our relations with the central committee system and the Cabinet Office itself, and to this end I negotiated with Sir John a carefully drafted list of 'ground rules' which were circulated to senior officials towards the end of April 1974. It enjoined the Cabinet Office, the CRPS and the Central Statistical Office to assist the Unit 'with advice and information to the maximum extent possible'. The outline stated that I would not normally be a member of official committees but that if I wanted myself or my staff to attend or receive papers 'there should be a disposition to say yes'. (In practice I attended not only any official committees I chose, but also all Cabinet Committees with the Prime Minister in the Chair, many Cabinet Committees with other Ministers in the Chair, and some full Cabinets. I also attended the weekly meetings of Deputy Secretaries in the Cabinet Office to determine the Government's future programme – but I never managed to get into the weekly mandarin summit of Permanent Secretaries held every Wednesday morning under the chairmanship of the then head of the Civil Service, Sir Douglas Allen.) In return for these very important concessions concerning the Unit's access to the Whitehall machine, I was formally required to promise that I would not 'show papers of Official Committees to the Prime Minister or report the views of individual officials to him'. This was 'not just to preserve the freedom of official discussion of issues at a preliminary stage but more importantly to respect the position of departmental Ministers' and I always respected that condition. The Cabinet Secretary was also very concerned that the Policy Unit's role should not affect his personal channels of communication to the Prime Minister or his function of providing a steering brief for the Prime Minister as Chairman of Cabinet Committees. He therefore issued instructions that copies of Cabinet Office briefs should not be sent to me. In fact I could always slip down to Private Office to read them and if necessary add my own covering brief – and the Private Secretaries often alerted me when a controversial Cabinet Office brief had arrived and they felt that something extra from the Policy Unit would be helpful to the Prime Minister. The agreement which Sir John and I reached concluded with a statement from him to his officials that 'we must therefore work closely together and make a success of it'. Both sides did their utmost to ensure this. The formal access guaranteed by this document was a major advance on anything achieved before. However, it was a privilege conceded only to members of the Downing Street Policy Unit and did not apply in every respect to other departmental special advisers working to individual Ministers in Whitehall. The latter were more restricted in access and were limited in number to two per Minister after December 1974. There was a proposal from the Minister responsible for the Civil Service in April 1974 to appoint me formally as head of all the special advisers in Whitehall; but I declined on the basis that it would give me responsibility for people over whom I had no control.

The most important contribution of the Policy Unit to central government was that it increased the Prime Minister's capacity for effective intervention in other Ministers' policy areas, for which more than mere personal will-power and the status of Downing Street is required, especially in the field of economic policy. It is simply not possible to maintain a sustained influence over economic policy without conducting a long, high-level and successful debate with the Treasury. Prime Ministers do, of course, have the ultimate power to overrule the Chancellor and insist on particular policies, which Mr Wilson did in 1975 when rejecting the Treasury's proposals for a statutory pay policy and Mr Callaghan did in 1976 when insisting on his own modest IMF package; Mrs Thatcher also is reported to have intervened on several occasions, particularly when amending the Treasury's 1981 budget. Under democratic Cabinet government, however, such an arbitrary approach is not one that a prudent Prime Minister would for long pursue, or a self-respecting Chancellor for long allow. Following such a path, a Prime Minister would soon consume his capital reserves of goodwill with his Cabinet colleagues. In Britain, as in the United States and most electorally accountable democracies, government involves a lengthy process of argument. In establishing the Policy Unit in Downing Street, Harold Wilson added significantly to the Prime Minister's fire-power in the policy-making process, and, indeed, the Policy Unit played a central role in the prime ministerial interventions in the crises of 1975, 1976 and 1979. This was only possible because the staff supporting me were of outstanding calibre. Each was required to have a rare combination of intellectual and political skills. As a single adviser covered one departmental policy area, the work-load on individuals was enormous. They needed the knowledge and intelligence to monitor and combat a whole department. (Our battles with the Treasury were basically conducted over those five and a half years by three remarkable economists, Gavyn Davies, Andrew Graham and David Piachaud.) I always recruited acknowledged policy experts of intellectual distinction because otherwise departments would not respect them or bother to include them in policy discussions. In addition they needed to have good political instincts, as the political dimension was one which mattered greatly to the Prime Minister; such instincts the regular civil service might either lack or, for professional reasons, prefer to leave to those with overt political commitments. The ultimate difference between us special advisers and the regular civil servants was that we alone were held directly responsible for the Prime Minister's policies in the sense that we shared his electoral fate if they failed – as indeed happened to me after the 1979 general election when I joined the ranks of the unemployed for five months.

I shall not write at length about either the Press Office or the Political Office because I had no direct professional experience of working in either. Under Harold Wilson I worked very closely with his Press Officer, Joe Haines. Joe was the toughest, funniest and most loyal colleague I have ever known and he is a man of total integrity. He knows the Fleet Street press inside out and handled them in exactly the way Harold Wilson wanted – which was quite roughly at times. However, his role in No. 10 went further than just dealing with the media. He possessed remarkable political insight and judgment and for most of the 1974–6 period he was effectively the Prime Minister's main political adviser. In my time he also wrote nearly every word of virtually all of Harold Wilson's public (as opposed to his parliamentary) speeches. But each Press Secretary in Downing Street, together with his half a dozen staff, does the job in his own way. Joe Haines's successor when James Callaghan took office, Tom McCaffrey, was more the civil servant, keeping a lower profile and not attempting to have the same political or policy influences with Mr Callaghan which Joe had enjoyed with Mr Wilson. Under Mrs Thatcher, Bernard Ingham has allegedly played a strong role in trying to manipulate the media and has even at times given the impression of being an independent source of political decision-making inside No. 10. It is very difficult to generalise about the Press Office as its methods reflect the different wishes of various Prime Ministers and the different styles of numerous Press Secretaries. There is, however, no doubt about its importance. All Prime Ministers, whatever they say in public, care passionately about how they are treated in the media. As far as they are concerned, the Press Secretary is a most important servant who has ready access at any time.

The Political Office can likewise be run in different ways, although much of its work concerns relations with the Prime Minister's party, at national and parliamentary and at constituency level, and is therefore not always visible to other officials within Downing Street. The Political Office is important because it reflects the crucial fact that the Prime Minister is still a partisan leader as well as head of the nation's government and he has to ride both horses at the same time. It is politically imprudent for a Prime Minister to be beguiled by the calls of national interest into completely abandoning his party political base – he must never forget that without the party he would never have reached Downing Street in the first place. The job of Political Secretary requires good political contacts at all levels, an ability to keep open many lines of party communication, and skill in protecting the Prime Minister's weak spots. Under Mr Callaghan, Tom McNally managed this successfully, as well as maintaining most amiable relations with the rest of No. 10. In addition, he often participated constructively in the discussions of the Policy Unit.

There are, of course, extra arms to the Prime Minister's advisory capability which are situated outside Downing Street. The Central Statistical Office – created by Harold Wilson after the 1964 election to improve the numeracy of the regular civil service – is part of that central capability. However, most important of the services provided to the Prime Minister from outside No. 10 are those from the Cabinet Office.

The Cabinet Office is directly adjacent to No. 10, although its main entrance is in Whitehall. There is a door between the two buildings which is kept locked – only the Cabinet Secretary on the one side and the No. 10 Private Office on the other have keys. The Cabinet Office's basic task is to co-ordinate and ensure the smooth running of Whitehall's official policy-making and administrative machinery. It also currently has the main responsibility for administering the civil service since Mrs Thatcher abolished the elephantine Civil Service department, dividing the responsibility between the Cabinet Office and (for pay and rations) the Treasury. Whether the Cabinet Secretary as the Prime Minister's most senior personal adviser should also run the civil service is seriously questionable – although it must be admitted that in my time the Civil Service Department was an equally imperfect solution.

The Cabinet Office existed originally simply to service the mechanics of government policy-making, including providing the secretariat for Cabinet and Cabinet meetings, issuing agendas and producing minutes. The Cabinet Secretary is the only person who institutionalises and reconciles the legitimate departmental conflicts of interest and differences of policy view which inevitably exist in Whitehall. This vital function of organising the machinery of central government is still conducted. Early in each week the Cabinet Office Secretariat issue the Cabinet Secretary with their proposals for Cabinet and Cabinet Committee business over the following fortnight. (This is supplemented periodically by what is called a 'Forward Look' which carries the same exercise forward for a period of up to six months.) Later in the week – usually on Thursday mornings during Cabinet – the Private Secretary to the Cabinet Secretary goes to No. 10 and establishes a programme in discussion with the two Private Secretaries who work on the Prime Minister's personal and parliamentary diaries. This constitutes the provisional programme of Cabinet business and Cabinet Committees to be chaired over the next two or three weeks. This draft programme is then discussed at a meeting which I and the Principal Private Secretary from Downing Street normally attended in the Cabinet Office under the Cabinet Secretary's chairmanship with his Deputy Secretaries late on Thursday or early on Friday. In the light of that discussion the Cabinet Secretary produces a forward programme of Cabinet, Cabinet Committee and official committee business which is sent to the Prime Minister, who in turn normally discusses it with his advisers and his Chief Whip on Friday morning. The Prime Minister's comments and conclusions are embodied in the specific arrangements which are then made for government business in the following week.

Apart from this purely administrative role, however, the Cabinet Office has over the years, perhaps inevitably, acquired an independent policy-making function. This tendency was accelerated during the Second World War when a section of economic advisers was located in the Cabinet Office; and again in the 1970s when Mr Heath established the Central Policy Review Staff (regrettably abolished by Mrs Thatcher in 1983) to carry out independent policy analysis for the Cabinet.

At the head of the Cabinet Office is the Cabinet Secretary who is usually the single most powerful official in Whitehall or indeed in the country. Although technically, and still often in practice, servicing the Cabinet, the Cabinet Secretary naturally works closely with the Prime Minister and, as such, and being a senior Permanent Secretary, he was, and still is, the most senior official working directly to the Prime Minister, as nobody in No. 10 in my time was above the level of Deputy Secretary. Under both Mr Wilson and Mr Callaghan the Cabinet Secretary was Sir John, now Lord, Hunt, who was impressively efficient and very effective at ensuring that the Whitehall machine delivered what the Prime Minister wanted.

There are certain ambiguities in the Cabinet Secretary's responsibilities which emerged clearly during the Labour Governments of the 1970s. First was the uncertainty already referred to, as to whether the Cabinet Office should be concerned simply with administration – with making the wheels of Whitehall turn smoothly – or whether it had an independent policy role. In practice, led by an ambitious Cabinet Secretary, backed by a swelling staff of over 500, and particularly aided by the CPRS, the Cabinet Office clearly exercised policy influence. This influence may be seen daily in the briefing papers which the Cabinet Secretary submits to the Chairmen of Cabinet Committees, and especially to the Prime Minister as Chairman of Cabinet. These briefs contain skilful advice on how to conduct the meeting, bearing in mind the interests and preferences of ministerial members. However, they have also increasingly contained arguments steering the Prime Minister towards one policy conclusion rather than another (usually prefaced by appropriate courtesies such as 'you may wish to . . .'). This is why the Policy Unit often found it necessary to submit its own briefing relating to the Cabinet Secretary's briefs. The increase in the policy influence of the Cabinet Office caused displeasure to some departmental Ministers who often complained to me about the intrusion of this extra policy arm. There were even occasional tensions between the Cabinet Office and the Policy Unit.

A similar ambiguity arose concerning whether the Cabinet Secretary's prime responsibility lay to the Cabinet as a collective whole or personally to the Prime Minister, on whose right hand he always sits in Cabinet. It can be argued that there should be no problem here since the Prime Minister is both Chairman and part of the Cabinet. However, political life is not as simple as that. At times the Prime Minister has personal interests which do not necessarily coincide with those of all his Cabinet colleagues. The Prime Minister might wish to restrain the policy activities of certain Cabinet colleagues, in which case he would want to influence the pace and way in which these were handled by the Whitehall machine. He might even wish to keep these issues from coming to Cabinet and also to influence which departments were or were not represented on the Cabinet Committees which discussed them. He would then use the Cabinet Secretary to achieve this – as Tony Benn periodically complained of during 1974–9. The Cabinet Secretary is, of course, supposed to serve the whole Cabinet but, in practice, where there is a conflict between the Prime Minister's interests and a Cabinet Minister's interests, he is always tempted to give priority to his final master and centre of power, the Prime Minister, who in any case might be said to be the ultimate definer of what is in the Cabinet's true interest.

This leads naturally into the third ambiguity concerning the Cabinet Secretary, which is whether he, or the Principal Private Secretary who runs the Downing Street Private Office, is actually the Prime Minister's primary official adviser. Certainly the Cabinet Secretary, Sir John Hunt, had ambitions and claims to be Mr Wilson's and Mr Callaghan's chief adviser. He was a senior Permanent Secretary, the only senior Permanent Secretary within the Prime Minister's central capability. He ranked above everybody in No. 10 and he commanded the Whitehall machine. However, although he had the status, he was not based at No. 10 and he did not therefore have automatic access to the Prime Minister. The Cabinet Secretary by convention had to telephone the Principal Private Secretary in order to receive clearance to come through the locked door to No. 10. On the other hand, the Principal Private Secretary – who in 1974–9 was first Robert Armstrong and then Kenneth Stowe – was always either an Under-Secretary or a Deputy Secretary. He therefore had the access but not the seniority. Watching the relations between the distinguished Cabinet Secretary and the rising Principal Private Secretary was absolutely fascinating. It was a game about territory. Some of the boundaries were clearly defined, not least by the locked green baize door between the two offices. But there was a grey area of common land which each sought to occupy. This led to subtleties of behaviour and finesse of language which aroused my amused admiration: the total courtesies of address; the softly veiled hints of status from the Cabinet Secretary when telephoning to say 'I am coming through to see the Prime Minister about a highly important and secret issue, but of course I am phoning to let you know'; the politely deferential tone of the Principal Private Secretary to his senior, while even so sometimes stating, 'This is not a convenient time but I will give you a ring when he is ready to see you.' Only the authors of the television series 'Yes, Prime Minister' could fully convey the delightful nuances of some of these exchanges. On the important issues, of course, these officials usually worked together in impressive tandem, serving both of my Prime Ministers to their great satisfaction. However, the status relationships and ambiguities at the margin led to perennial tension, which Mr Wilson always relished and seemed occasionally to provoke.

These unresolved questions of authority in the centre of British government relate directly to the continuing debate about whether there should or should not be a separate and permanent Prime Minister's department. At present not only are the staff at No. 10 small in numbers but also most of the senior advisers are temporary: the regular civil servants in the Private Office or the Press Office are on two- to three-year loan from other departments and the political aides are outsiders brought in on short-term contracts. This practice has been felt by some critics to lack the strengths of continuity. It could also be a problem that officials on loan from the Treasury or the Foreign Office might come under pressure from their home departments (bearing in mind that their long-term future promotion prospects lie in those departments) to press the departmental view on the Prime Minister. However, I am bound to say that in my time this seemed to be a problem only occasionally with the Foreign Office side. In fact the Downing Street officials served both Prime Ministers with enormous devotion and loyalty – and even courage in the case of those on loan from the Treasury.

It might be that a permanent Prime Minister's department would be a better, certainly a tidier, alternative. Indeed, in 1977–8 Mr Callaghan played with the idea while considering a major reorganisation of central government. In practice, however, the Prime Minister does under the existing system have all the advisory facilities he needs, even though they may be scattered a little untidily around central government. As Mr Callaghan concluded after his own examination of this question, 'You know, I can pull all the levers I want and it does not matter too much whether the signals go into No. 10 or into the Cabinet Office, or into the Lord Privy Seal's office or wherever.' In its favour, the present *ad hoc* system avoids the bureaucracy, the hierarchy and the inflation of numbers which would certainly accompany the creation of a separate permanent department. It also means that the Prime Minister does not have to waste much time on 'departmental problems'.

At present No. 10 is small, efficient, and non-hierarchical, with anybody being allowed to make a contribution to the Prime Minister if he or she has something helpful to say. The present set-up in No. 10 works well when there is a Prime Minister in residence who knows how to pull the levers and operate the system. Provided that the personalities do not clash inside that small political kitchen, the system is flexible and leaves a Prime Minister free to use it when and however he wants to. Certainly both Mr Wilson and Mr Callaghan knew how to make use of the advisory system available to them. If they wanted to intervene on policy matters they had the advisory ammunition available to do so with good effect.

While considering how the central Whitehall machine works it would be remiss to omit the Treasury, which during those difficult five years bore the brunt of the day-to-day management of a sickly economy under a government with ambitious electoral commitments, and then as yet without the cushion of massive oil revenues which later made life so much easier (for the government if not for the unemployed) under Mrs Thatcher. Much of the later narrative is concerned with Downing Street's role in economic crises. However, economic policy in Britain is the primary concern of Her Majesty's Treasury, situated on the corner block of Whitehall and Great George Street. Most of any British government's analysis of economic policy – and virtually all the official papers devoted to it – is generated along the high curving corridors of that appropriately sombre building. Internally the Treasury is separated under Deputy Secretaries into divisions which conduct the various sub-strata of economic policy: domestic, overseas, monetary, public sector, industrial etc. (this list is illustrative rather than comprehensive). These mini-kingdoms may rise or fall in importance, or extend or contract their subject boundaries, according to present fashion or the priorities of the government of the day.

In the twentieth century, with the increase of central government intervention in the nation's affairs, the Treasury's overall power and functions have steadily and significantly expanded – as have its numbers, although it still remains small in relation to the rest of Whitehall. The Treasury has long been and remains today the pre-eminent domestic department. At the political/ministerial level the Chancellor is in principle – and normally in practice – the most senior domestic departmental minister. He is the most powerful because he controls the resources available to other Ministers – although the variable circumstances of an individual Chancellor's personality, or of his party or national influence, could conceivably leave a Home Secretary or Foreign Secretary colleague with more effective political powers at a given time.

During 1974–9 the Chancellor was Denis Healey, a robust

North Countryman whose extrovert and occasionally brutal style reflected formidable physical and mental stamina. Despite his self-image of being a 'simple man' and his earthy language, Denis Healey is an intellectual of Renaissance range who is able to converse in several languages about philosophy, music, literature and art, and is a photographer of professional level. In fact, during his term as Chancellor his intellectual grasp was superior to his political sensitivity and he at times appeared touchingly innocent about the political implications of his economic policies. To his great credit he never plotted, schemed or intrigued and was totally loyal to both his Prime Ministers. Perhaps this absence of political guile, together with his lack of interest or skill in leading any tribal faction or even identifying closely with any particular wing of the Labour party, explains his failure to achieve the leadership after Mr Callaghan retired. In terms of contribution and national stature, however, he was worthy of being elected leader. During his years as Chancellor he was a major Cabinet figure, widely respected by his colleagues. Neither of his Prime Ministers found it easy to impose upon him changes of economic policy. They had to convince him intellectually and politically and to do that they needed firm conviction and a well-argued case.

The Treasury officials who served the Chancellor during the 1970s are occasionally subject to gentle criticism in the ensuing chapters of this book, certainly with just cause in a few particular instances. They can also be criticised in general for creating a departmental culture of monastic unworldliness. They appear to spend too much of their lives mixing only with other Treasury men. They are often foolishly proud of being untainted or uncorrupted by contact with or practical knowledge of the soiled outside world into whose fiscal and monetary affairs they intervene with devastating effect. However, these are only small black marks in the margin. Overall British Treasury men represent the cream of administrations by any international test or criteria. Treasury officials are chosen from the highest calibre of applicants to the central bureaucracy. Their ability is very high and they rightly dominate British central government. This intellectual dominance is assisted by a shrewd policy of territorial colonisation across Whitehall. Able Treasury men are placed in senior positions in other Whitehall departments, as well as on the staff of the Prime Minister in Downing Street and of the Governor of the Bank of England. Even after thus transferring, on my observation, the Treasury culture continues to condition its employees' approach to government problems and policies. Once a Treasury man always a Treasury man. Nor is that necessarily a bad thing. As a special adviser, arriving from the outside academic world into a suspicious Whitehall environment, I personally found the Treasury men ultimately the most open and satisfactory to deal with. Admittedly it is also true that some of my most brutal bureaucratic battles (ignoring the bizarre fratricide within one Prime Minister's own personal team) were with the Treasury. However, once Treasury officials were convinced that an adviser intended to be a serious player in the Whitehall game – and successfully carried some policy clout with his or her own Minister – I found that they opened up and responded. They did so with none of the irritatingly snooty hostility to outside expertise which too often characterises those in Whitehall's lower layers and lesser Ministries who apparently, and perhaps justifiably, feel most threatened by able intruders. As is so often the case in life, it is ultimately easiest to deal with the best.

A final reflection upon the quality of advice available to the Prime Minister from within central government concerns the continuing health and durability of the British system of Cabinet government. There has been much press and academic speculation on the demise of the Cabinet as an effective, as opposed to a dignified, institution. Harold Wilson was supposed to have undermined it fatally by his 'presidential' style in the 1960s. Mrs Thatcher has allegedly finished it off by using the Cabinet as a mere rubber stamp to process her own authoritarian decisions. The resignations of Francis Pym in 1983 and Michael Heseltine in 1986 specifically referred to Mrs Thatcher's high-handed style of taking major decisions without fully consulting Cabinet. However, during the period of the 1974–9 Labour Governments the full Cabinet together with its Cabinet Committees were effectively the central instruments of government policy on the main issues. All major decisions (except those concerning highly sensitive discussions on monetary intentions or defence technology) were fully debated in the Cabinet room. Although each Prime Minister intervened successfully to influence and leave his personal imprint on various policy decisions, each worked through the Cabinet system and was always aware of the need to carry Cabinet colleagues.

Mr Wilson and Mr Callaghan in particular believed in principle that the Cabinet (and its Committees) ought to be involved and should have a full say in the major issues of the day. Both men had been members of Cabinet long before becoming Prime Minister; both valued its contribution and believed in collective responsibility. Full and proper use of the Cabinet also had practical political attractions to a Prime Minister. When a decision has been taken – especially one that is politically unpopular – it is very helpful if a couple of dozen senior politicians can go back to the governing party in the Commons and say to worried backbenchers, 'Well, we discussed it thoroughly, and the points and criticisms which you make were quite rightly presented and fully argued, but in the end we felt that it was on balance best to take this different course.' It is certainly not helpful to the Prime Minister or the government for it to be said, as it was when Michael Heseltine resigned in 1986 over the Westland affair, that Cabinet was not given a proper chance to discuss the issue.

A Prime Minister is a party politician who may not always be absolutely certain of his or her own political base. The Prime Minister does not like to drift too far apart from senior colleagues, some of whom are competing for the job in No. 10, perhaps waiting for the leader to become isolated and then make a mistake. It is admittedly possible for a Prime Minister – especially when his or her personal star is high, as, for example, after a big election victory – to pre-empt a Cabinet decision by announcing a strong policy preference to colleagues in advance of discussion. Mrs Thatcher has allegedly done that at times, especially during the early years of her tenure of Downing Street. However, Mr Wilson and Mr Callaghan did not normally adopt that posture (when the latter finally and decisively showed his hand over the IMF at the end of 1976 it was only after prolonged collective discussion). If it is done too often, senior colleagues will resent it and may eventually combine to defeat the Prime Minister in Cabinet, which undermines prime ministerial authority. Alternatively, resentful Ministers may resign or be forced out, strengthening the discontent on the Government's own backbenches – something Mrs Thatcher did until there was almost more political weight on the back than on her front benches. A Prime Minister should not go out on a limb too often in Cabinet. He or she is after all the Chairman, and therefore needs to retain the trust of colleagues that the Chairman will sum up their opinions fairly. It is therefore helpful during a major dispute to consult interested colleagues personally beforehand to try to establish a consensus, or at least to establish the real areas of disagreement, as Mr Callaghan usually did. Mr Callaghan was especially careful to conduct his personal arguments with Chancellor Healey privately in his study; then, having usually secured some concessions from the Treasury, he was able fully to support his Chancellor publicly in the Cabinet room. Mr Callaghan also assiduously kept Michael Foot fully in the picture, thus helping to ensure that the left wing did not detach in united opposition to his tough economic measures. Mr Wilson set a similar example earlier, always consulting closely with Mr Callaghan and Mr Foot during 1974–6.

The impression I received of the continuing strength of the system of Cabinet government may of course have been a little exaggerated because of the high quality of the Cabinet Ministers involved (Mr Wilson's 1974–6 Cabinet contained all Labour's Chancellors from 1964–79). The introduction in 1974 of special advisers working to most Cabinet Ministers was another factor which improved the quality of Cabinet debate at that time. It meant that, ideally, Ministers received high-level briefing on fields of policy outside those for which they were departmentally responsible. This was especially important during the IMF crisis, when it was striking how wide a range of Ministers contributed to the discussions. This applied to the younger ones in particular – Hattersley, Owen, Rodgers and Williams – but included more senior spokesmen such as Lever, Shore, Benn, and of course the Prime Minister, all of whom were assisted by qualified economists as special advisers. By contrast, the minority of Ministers who were often silent – including Peart, Mason and Mellish – had in general chosen not to employ special advisers. Indeed, the regular civil servants in the Private Office often mentioned to me that the introduction of a system of special advisers had altered the way in which Cabinet worked by producing much wider debate. Conversely, Mr Heath's earlier discussions of economic policy apparently rarely involved as many as half a dozen Ministers. The latter example may also have reflected differences of prime ministerial personality (and of attitude between the Conservative and Labour Parties towards critical argument). There is, however, no doubt that involving Cabinet Ministers in debate is healthy for the Cabinet system. Having economics policy analysts as special advisers certainly enabled non-economist Ministers to participate intelligently in Cabinet economic discussions.

The economic and social policy fields gave most scope for such wide-ranging Cabinet debate. By contrast, the remoter areas of foreign policy were usually covered quickly and without interruption during the Foreign Secretary's routine survey early on the agenda of most Thursday morning Cabinets (Rhodesia and Belize were frequent items in the 1970s, while the Falkland Islands also came up three times and were quickly passed over).

Doubts have been raised as to whether the Cabinet has been kept as well informed under Conservative administrations in the 1980s. It is particularly interesting to compare Mrs Thatcher's autocratic handling of her Cabinet during the Westland affair in 1986 with the crises occurring under Mr Wilson and Mr Callaghan which are described later in this book. The following chapters therefore examine the nature of prime ministerial power in practice by examining the day-to-day working of government in major areas of policy.

2

Into Downing Street, March 1974

Having outlined the structure of government in Downing Street and Whitehall, it may be helpful to describe how I became involved in the first place. The main explanation lies in the two most important factors in the majority of political careers: chance and availability. At the end of 1973 Harold Wilson was looking for someone to monitor his personal opinion polls. He intended to employ Robert Worcester's market research firm MORI to conduct a survey of public opinion but he wanted someone to supervise these polls on his behalf from the Labour party's political point of view. I had met the then Labour leader only twice previously (once at a City lunch and once when interviewing him for a biography I was writing on Herbert Morrison), but after making enquiries he invited me to help him. My job as a university lecturer (in the less demanding days of the early 1970s) provided sufficient spare time for me to be available.

We planned to carry out monthly opinion polls over the following years up to the next election which was legally due by June 1975. The results of the first poll were ready and analysed at the beginning of February 1974. We were scheduled to meet with Mr Wilson for lunch on Thursday 7 February to discuss the poll but when Bob Worcester and I reached the House of Commons he asked us to wait until after lunch because a major event had intervened – Edward Heath had just dissolved Parliament, sixteen months before its term. When we met after lunch to discuss our poll it was in the new context of the election campaign immediately ahead. At the conclusion of our discussions Mr Wilson said to me, 'We will meet again on Sunday.' We therefore met on Sunday 10 February and at the end of that

FIRST LORD

1   Harold Wilson returns to No. 10 at the start of a new term in office
as Prime Minister in February 1974.

2 Harold Wilson with Roy Jenkins, disappointed to be sent back to the Home Office.

3 Harold Wilson with Marcia Williams (later Lady Falkender), for twenty years his Political Secretary.

4 Merlyn Rees, Secretary of State for Northern Ireland, leaving No.10 in July 1984.

5 The terrible twins of the TUC – Hugh Scanlon of the engineers and Jack Jones of the transport workers.

6 Marcia Falkender and Bernard Donoughue, competitors in the 'Kitchen Cabinet' in 1974.

7 The Prime Minister with his Press Secretary and candid friend, Joe Haines.

meeting, and every day after that throughout the campaign, he said, 'I will see you tomorrow.' In this way I became part of Mr Wilson's small personal entourage which managed his election victory and subsequently joined him in Downing Street when he became Prime Minister.

There were four central figures in the Labour leader's personal team. Most important in terms of political brilliance and daily practical contribution was Joe Haines, now the Political Editor of the Mirror Newspaper Group, who had worked as Mr Wilson's Press Officer, speech writer and political adviser since the late 1960s. The person with potentially the most personal influence – if only intermittently exercised – over Harold Wilson (especially on minor non-policy matters) was Marcia Williams, now Lady Falkender, who had been his Political Secretary for nearly twenty years. The day-to-day running of the leader's office under Mrs Williams's fitful authoritarian command was left to Albert, subsequently Lord, Murray, a former Labour junior Minister who had lost his seat in 1970 (and later died in 1980). I was the fourth of the inner core of aides who worked together full-time throughout the campaign and had total access to Mr Wilson. Other experienced people were involved periodically, including the late Lord Balogh, a distinguished economist, Peter (later Lord) Lovell-Davies, who was successful in public relations, and two former Labour MPs, Terry Boston and Ben Whitaker. Apart from Joe Haines and Marcia Williams, the central four had changed slightly from those who had been close to Mr Wilson in the previous campaign of 1970. But others, such as Peter Shore and Gerald Kaufman, who had been central to the earlier campaign, were now in Parliament and busily occupied fighting in their own constituencies.

It was always said in the press that Harold Wilson was surrounded by a group of 'lackeys'. I assumed that was the case when joining the team, but actually it was far from the truth. Naturally, advisers working on the personal staff of a party leader will, and should, show polite deference to their employer in front of outsiders. However, it was a curious aspect of Mr Wilson's tolerant and apparently masochistic character that he always invited contradiction and harsh comments in private from those working close to him. Marcia Williams was often humiliatingly severe as well as perceptive in her remarks, and Joe Haines was totally incapable of being a lackey to anyone – in fact he is something of a specialist in dissent through the honest barbed comment. On my daily observation during that campaign and subsequently in government, he was courageous and said absolutely what he thought, however unwelcome it may be to the recipient. He strongly opposed many of Mr Wilson's less felicitous ideas in private – and then, if overruled, of course had to defend them in public to disapproving fellow journalists.

The February 1974 election was launched by Prime Minister Heath on the main issue of the miners' strike and the underlying theme of 'Who governs Britain?' In the background were deeper problems. Inflation was for the first time since the war rising towards double figures, and looming behind that was the first oil crisis of 1973. Looking back, what is striking in that election campaign is how few participants from any side fully understood the true significance of the recent energy crisis – perhaps only Edward Heath in the government and Harold Lever on the Labour side. The economic arguments used in the actual campaign were primarily concerned with the problem of the miners' strike and the undoubted failings of the Conservative Chancellor, Anthony Barber. Little light was thrown on how the next Government, Labour or Conservative, would cope with the appalling economic implications of recent developments in the Middle East.

Mr Wilson's election team established Labour's campaign strategy on Sunday 10 February in the leader's house at 5 Lord North Street. After a long discussion, Mr Wilson stood up and said that it was quite clear that this election would be just like the seventeenth-century English Civil War. He described in impressive detail the battle of Marston Moor and said he was going to fight his campaign in the manner of Oliver Cromwell. During the first week the Conservative attack would be contained; and in the second week Labour would counter-attack by asserting its better economic policies, its commitment to social consensus through the social contract, and above all its plans to reduce prices. In the third week there would be skirmishes on the flanks, exploiting Enoch Powell's expected attacks on the Conservative leadership over the question of EEC membership. Although events in an election cannot be precisely forecast or controlled, we broadly followed this strategy. The weapons used were predominantly the speeches of Mr Wilson, his television and radio broadcasts, and his press conference statements. These were usually written by Joe Haines, sometimes helped by me. The topics and themes to be emphasised on these occasions were planned in advance by the team in order to try to focus the media debates and the political argument on the issues which we wanted discussed: basically, prices, the Social Contract and the need for better economic management. We were not always successful in this and inevitably there were setbacks. We could not control the media; most national daily newspapers (the *Financial Times*, the *Daily Mirror* and the *Guardian* being distinguished exceptions) then as now were predominantly owned and/or edited by aggressive supporters of the Conservative party who during elections saw their products more as vehicles for political propaganda than as purveyors of accurate news. Hence they repeatedly ignored Mr Wilson's speeches and continued to present the campaign in terms of the Conservative theme of 'Who governs Britain?'. However, the television gave reasonably fair coverage (certainly ITV did) and the 9 o'clock news on BBC television and the 10 o'clock news on ITV became crucial instruments in our campaign. Our selected daily theme and slogan were written into the central part of each evening's main speech given by Mr Wilson. In the media handout the parts of the speech which he wished to be emphasised were underlined and the speech was timed conveniently to be filmed for those television news programmes. It was therefore possible to project our main arguments into most homes each evening regardless of the fact that the *Daily Mail*, the *Daily Express*, the *Sun*, *The Times* and the *Daily Telegraph* were effectively being published from Conservative Central Office. In Britain television has become an essential instrument for any non-Conservative party attempting to influence the election debate.

Turning to the actual conduct of the campaign, there were four important developments in the third week which required tactical reactions from our team. One concerned the miners: on

21 February the Pay Board announced that their investigations showed that miners' wages had previously been miscalculated and understated. This made it possible for us to argue that the whole battle with the miners need not have happened and had been brought about by incompetence in government. Actually a friendly journalist had alerted our team in advance of this announcement and we were able to brief Mr Wilson beforehand with the background facts. He made a big play with the issue, both in his evening speech and on television, whereas the Conservatives were uncharacteristically less efficient. Apparently nobody at Conservative headquarters saw the significance of the announcement and consequently Mr Heath on television seemed to be out of touch and unable to answer the journalists' questions.

Mr Enoch Powell also became an issue. He made three major speeches over the final weekend of the campaign. In the last one, on Monday 25 February, he explicitly called upon the electorate to vote Labour because he preferred its sceptical position on the EEC. It is perhaps difficult now to recall the importance of Enoch Powell in the Conservative party at that time. He was the dissident leader of the disenchanted right wing, and he had great influence among working-class Tories, particularly in the Midlands where there were many marginal seats. Mr Powell was in regular contact with Mr Wilson's team during February 1974, always using the journalist Andrew Alexander as intermediary. The latter alerted us to the content of Mr Powell's speeches and we planned that Mr Wilson's statements over that weekend would dovetail with them, by emphasising Labour's scepticism about the Common Market. Thus we exploited the confusion created by Mr Powell among Conservative voters.

The trade figures were published on the same Monday as Enoch Powell's final speech, three days before the poll. We did not know for sure that they would be bad, but planned our strategy on the assumption that they might be (and they were). It was arranged that the full Labour economic team – Healey as Shadow Chancellor, Jenkins and Callaghan as previous Chancellors, Wilson as Prime Minister, and Shore as an economics spokesman – be present at the press conference the following morning. This required careful pre-planning because in an election campaign senior party figures have many prior speaking engagements and cannot be gathered together at the last moment. The press conference on the trade figures made a good impact in demonstrating the quality and depth of economic experience within Labour's economic team.

The dramatic late upsurge in support for the Liberals also required assessment and reaction from Mr Wilson's team. We concluded firstly that people were being driven to support the centre party by irritation at the personal wrangling between the two major party leaders; and secondly that in terms of parliamentary seats the Liberal revival was more damaging to the Conservatives than to Labour. Therefore Mr Wilson was advised to stop attacking Mr Heath personally and then to enjoy the benefits of the Liberal intervention.

On balance these tactical issues arising in the final week of the campaign were handled to Labour's advantage. Of course not everything fell our way; indeed, a number of operations handled by the Labour party organisation, then located in Transport House in Smith Square, went sadly, if often hilariously, wrong. The arrangements for the party leader's meetings and of media coverage were often appalling. In the middle of the campaign Transport House completely ran out of paper and was therefore unable to print and issue enough press handouts (officials had failed to foresee that an election campaign would require extra paper). One of the better senior officials frequently broke down and wept. An early sign of his feeling stress was when he agitatedly took off his shoes in the middle of a committee or conference; a final sign was when he stormed out of the meeting in his socks. On the Friday after the election Mr Wilson flew back from his Liverpool constituency with his team while the final results were still being declared and the outcome was as yet unclear. On landing at Heathrow Airport he telephoned Transport House to discover whether the final results would confirm that there would be a Labour Government; however, nobody at party headquarters appeared to be following the results, in which they might have been presumed to have had an interest. Sadly, apart from the stalwart work carried out by the excellent and long-suffering Reg Underhill, much of the energy as existed in the then upper levels of Transport House was devoted to petty jealousies and internal squabbling, with little apparent concern for the need to unite in order to defeat the Conservatives. Fortunately it did not seem to matter very much. Indeed, the fact that Labour won two general elections in 1974 despite having a central organisation of almost unbelievable inefficiency raises interesting questions about the role and value of old-style party organisations in a modern electoral world dominated by television.

The daily schedule of the leader and his staff in the campaign was fairly repetitive. We met each morning at Mr Wilson's house in Lord North Street at around 8.00 am, by which time he had read the draft of that day's speech which we had left with him overnight. We then discussed any amendments he wished to make to the speech and also what should be emphasised in the press statement at that morning's press conference. At 9.00 am Mr Wilson went to the daily meeting of the Campaign Committee at Transport House. We would go with him to Smith Square but did not go into the committee room as it was an official party meeting, the purpose of which was said to be to give party dignitaries a sense of involvement rather than having any serious practical influence on the campaign. While Mr Wilson was in conference we would complete the statement for the late morning press conference. At around 10.00 am Mr Wilson would leave the Committee and either return to his home in Lord North Street or go to his personal office in Transport House, where we would finalise the day's speech and send it for typing and distribution. We also then agreed on the main theme of the next day's speech. After the press conference Mr Wilson usually left for his diary of meetings around the country and to deliver his daily major speech. Once he had gone, Joe Haines and I would go to our office in Transport House to write the first draft of the next day's speech. (With the help of taxis from Westminster to the Aldwych, I also managed to fit in my weekly routine of lectures and classes at the London School of Economics.) Therefore, by the time Mr Wilson returned at about midnight from Glasgow or some other mass meeting, we had the next day's speech in draft form and were waiting at Lord North Street to give it to him to read overnight ready to make comments in the morning. This was also the time when we would sit with him and talk over the day's events. I usually reached home in Kentish Town at around 2.00 am – and was back in Lord North Street by 8.00. It was a relentless daily routine, but it produced well-thought-out speeches in good time and served the leader efficiently.

Opinion polls were very important to the conduct of the Labour leader's campaign. Claims by politicians that they are not interested in or influenced by polls should be treated with scepticism. Mr Wilson followed Robert Worcester's private polls for the Labour party with great interest, even though they carried few shreds of comfort. In the middle of the first week Labour was 12 per cent behind the Conservatives in the private MORI polls and doing even worse in some of the other published surveys. That deficit then narrowed until the two parties were virtually level a week later, although then Labour began to slip away until it was 7–8 per cent behind. However, over the final weekend, during which time Enoch Powell made his anti-Heath speeches, the gap began to narrow again. In polling terms, what was most encouraging to me was that Labour began to take the lead with the policy issues on which we were laying most stress (prices and social consensus). On this basis I advised Mr Wilson on the eve of polling day that he would be the next Prime Minister. However, Labour actually never once led in the polls on party choice during the entire February 1974 campaign. This may explain why so many Labour politicians thought that the party could not win. When I several times telephoned leading party figures to ask them to attend a morning press conference, it was apparent from the frequent lack of enthusiasm in their responses that many of them saw little point in participating as they believed we were going to lose anyway. In one sense they were not wholly wrong. Labour did not actually lead at the ballot box, being 0.8 per cent behind on votes polled. However, it secured a tiny majority in seats and therefore, once Mr Heath's attempt to seduce the Liberal leader Jeremy Thorpe into coalition failed, Mr Wilson was invited to form his third administration.

Harold Wilson had thus won his third election out of four. However, his personal hopes and morale had not been high.

Throughout the February campaign he was clearly worried, puzzled and even bewildered about what would be the result. Several times he said to me that he could 'not read' this election and that more than any previous one he had 'no feel' for how it was going. His confidence may have been undermined by the earlier 1970 campaign, which he thought he was winning although this was not in fact the case. He often said that this February campaign was his 'best organised' and 'happiest', and the one with the best speeches. (Apparently previous campaigns – as with that conducted eight months later in October 1974 – were blighted by administrative inefficiencies and hysterical tensions within the team.) None the less, he was often tired and edgy. It is very hard for an outsider to understand the tremendous strain imposed on a political leader during an election campaign. The work-load and pressure of that daily treadmill are enormous, and Mr Wilson showed many signs of tension and exhaustion. One of his eyes became infected and his voice strained. Late at night, when he returned for our meetings at 5 Lord North Street, he was utterly drained. He would slump in his chair, light a cigar and sip a brandy, his exhaustion showing as he talked over the day's events and the big evening meeting. Then he would pick up a little and we would give him the draft of the next day's speech. He always made some changes, almost as if he found it hard in principle to accept that other people were now writing his speeches for him.

On polling day, 28 February, Mr Wilson still clearly feared defeat and he had certainly made no preparations whatsoever for victory. On that evening I went with him for a final tour of the clubs and polling booths in his Huyton constituency. It was quite an eerie experience. On such a windy and wet night the outskirts of Liverpool seemed desolate and the small windswept figure of Mr Wilson looked disconsolate and out of place. Everyone thought we were losing and treated us accordingly, showing little interest in this tiny group of yesterday's men. The offhand attitude of the police was also interesting – they obviously did not think that they were escorting, and ought to be protecting, the next Prime Minister of Britain. Mr Wilson himself was clearly not very convinced when I told him that on the basis of the trend in our final private polls he could well lead the next government, if perhaps a minority one. On the contrary, he had made quite bizarre secret preparations to go into hiding should he be defeated. So that night, although Mr Wilson's team were all booked into the Adelphi Hotel in Liverpool, we switched at the last moment to the Golden Cross at Kirkby, then a very depressing little hotel. Although no one was supposed to know that we were there, somebody at the hotel immediately tipped off the press and twenty minutes later the tiny lobby was crowded with journalists. Shortly afterwards our team trooped sheepishly back to the Adelphi. We were still behaving like losers in hiding even though it now seemed that Labour had won.

We flew back to London from Liverpool in the middle of Friday 1 March believing that the election had finally gone our way. But several of the late results did not fall to Labour as expected, and by the time we reached Transport House towards teatime on Friday the outcome still looked very marginal. Mr Heath announced that he would hold talks with the other parties, which, as Labour clearly would not join in, meant trying to form a coalition with the Liberals. In response, Mr Wilson called the Shadow Cabinet together to discuss tactics and, after some desultory discussions, it was agreed that we should all go home and await the unfolding of events. Mr Wilson went to his farmhouse in Buckinghamshire and, after numerous telephone conversations between us over the weekend, the team gathered again at Lord North Street on Sunday evening, 3 March, to discuss tactics and to consider who should be in the new Labour Cabinet. Our assumption was that Mr Heath's coalition endeavour would fail and that Mr Wilson would form the next administration. This was confirmed late on Monday afternoon when Mr Wilson was summoned to Buckingham Palace and asked to form a Government. His closest personal advisers went with him to the Palace and we returned to enter Downing Street together in the early evening.

While in Liverpool Mr Wilson had told me that, if elected, he planned to be a very different Prime Minister from how he had been when first elected Prime Minister in 1964. There would this time be 'no presidential nonsense', no 'first hundred days', and no 'beer and sandwiches at No. 10' to solve crises. He said that Ministers would run their own departments and as Prime Minister he would try not to interfere. He used one of his familiar footballing analogies, saying that his role would be akin to that of a 'sweeper' in the defence rather than a 'striker' in attack. This indeed was the style he followed.

Mr Wilson began making Cabinet appointments immediately on that Monday evening. His new Cabinet was very orthodox; it was broadly in line with the previous Shadow Cabinet and was formed very much with party balance in mind. He was always conscious of party balance and whenever we discussed appointments he always sought to match the right and the left. One surprise promotion was that of Michael Foot to Employment (I suggested this to Mr Wilson at our discussion on Sunday evening, 3 March, but others may have thought of it as well). Roy Jenkins, offered the Home Office, seemed unhappy and did not accept until quite late. Roy was particularly worried about Peter Shore going to the Department of Trade as he was so hostile to the EEC. Education, which is not viewed as an important post either by politicians or by senior civil servants, was left vacant until the last minute (Education also did not appear on Labour's Cabinet agenda throughout the first year of office). The junior appointments were made in a very unsystematic way, often almost as an afterthought. There are many junior posts to be filled and a Prime Minister may not always know who are the best candidates among the young MPs. In some cases he accepts the suggestions of a departmental Minister, especially if the latter is a powerful political colleague. (James Callagham and Roy Jenkins effectively made their own junior appointments.) In March 1974 many of the other junior postings were chosen on the suggestions of Mr Wilson's personal staff at lunch.

In terms of ability and experience the Cabinet appointed by Mr Wilson in February 1974 was perhaps the most impressive in Britain in this century. As such it was in direct contrast to his first experience of entering Downing Street in 1964. This time, in the context of his footballing language, he had plenty of centre forwards. At the heart of his Cabinet were six very experienced politicians. James Callaghan, at the Foreign Office, had been in Parliament since 1945. He had first become a

Minister in 1949, then been made Chancellor of the Exchequer in 1964 and Home Secretary from 1967–70. Present on the National Executive Committee since the 1950s, he was a very powerful party as well as ministerial figure. Mr Callaghan worked very closely with Mr Wilson during the two years 1974–6. It was of crucial importance to the stability of this final Wilson administration that there were none of the jealousies between these two senior figures which had occasionally been evident in the 1960s. They discussed all important issues together and formed a very impressive political partnership.

The next major figure in the Cabinet was Roy Jenkins at the Home Office. He had been in Parliament for a quarter of a century and was also a very successful Chancellor of the Exchequer in 1967–70. In the public eye, and especially in the media, he was probably seen as the Labour heir apparent. However, he was already personally alienated from many of Labour's policies. In fact he appeared unconvinced that he wanted to go into the Government at all in 1974 – and returning to the Home Office where he had been an outstanding success in the mid-1960s was certainly a kind of demotion for a former Chancellor. Mr Wilson's view was that as Roy Jenkins had resigned from the Shadow Cabinet in 1972 because of his opposition to the party's scepticism over EEC membership, he could not immediately expect one of the plum jobs at the Exchequer or the Foreign Office. Although he had to be punished for that act of rebellion, he was undoubtedly a politician and statesman of international stature.

Denis Healey, appointed Chancellor of the Exchequer, had also been in the Commons for a quarter of a century. He was a successful Defence Secretary throughout the 1964–70 Government and he always demonstrated a formidable intelligence and incredible stamina. As Minister for the Environment Mr Wilson chose Anthony Crosland, the most celebrated intellectual in the post-war Labour party. He was a brilliant man to have around the Cabinet table as he was able to contribute to virtually all areas of policy, and he was especially good at placing policy discussions within the philosophical structure of a democratic socialist party.

The fifth major figure in the Cabinet was Barbara Castle at

Health and Social Security. One of the 1945 generation of parliamentarians, she was a leading party figure on the National Executive Committee and a very prominent Minister in the late 1960s. She was shrewd, aggressive and a long-standing political associate of Harold Wilson. By 1974 he seemed a little frightened of her; even bored by her increasing shrillness. Although she had been politically damaged by her earlier battles with the TUC over the 'In Place of Strife' debate, she was still a serious and energetic Minister.

Finally there was Tony Benn at the Department of Industry. He was more preoccupied with leading the left wing in the country than contributing to the Government's success in Whitehall and Westminster – indeed he cleverly managed to give the impression of being a member but not a supporter of the Labour Government. An able and skilful political operator, he was very effective both in Cabinet and in Parliament. He presented his arguments brilliantly and most impressive was the way that he never reacted to criticism or hostility from his Cabinet colleagues. At all times he remained cool and polite, simply restating his case over and over again. Whatever one's view of his policy positions, or his repeated blatant disloyalties to the Labour Government of which he was nominally a member, he was certainly a remarkable political figure.

With these heavy-weights were such other outstanding people as Harold Lever and Peter Shore. Standing apart in a different dimension was Michael Foot, perhaps not a great politician and sometimes not wholly interested in the hard details of economic policy, but a man of great honour, warmth, humour, culture and compassion, as well as the best rhetorician of his generation, who gave unwavering loyalty to Harold Wilson and James Callaghan throughout their 1974–9 administrations. If such a formidable Cabinet were not to succeed it would be because of the force of events or the deadweight of Labour's antique ideological commitments rather than deficiencies of human resources. Once assembled, they immediately set to work. The miners' strike was settled on Wednesday 6 March by simple if ominous capitulation. That eliminated, if it did not solve, the most immediate inherited policy problem and cleared the desk for Labour's new government.

3

Harold Wilson's Economic and Industrial Policy, 1974–5

To me as a newcomer to central government, the most striking feature of the first twelve months of Harold Wilson's third and fourth administrations was the infrequency of collective Cabinet discussions on economic policy. Indeed, I cannot recall a single sustained discussion in Cabinet or Cabinet Committee of central economic policy – of fiscal or monetary management, or any direct measures to curb public expenditure growth or wage inflation – until December 1974. Chancellor Healey did make a report to the Ministerial Committee on Economic Strategy in June 1974, but it did not produce any serious ministerial discussions or action. Between March and October 1974 the Prime Minister and the Cabinet were otherwise occupied, being wholly geared towards winning the inevitable second general election (which came in October). First, peace was settled with the miners. Then everybody was busy producing a flood of 'green papers', suggesting attractive policy propositions which were hopefully to be carried out by the Labour Government when re-elected with a clear majority. The legislative programme for the short parliamentary session ahead was worthy and reformist without being frighteningly extreme in view of another general election expected soon. Legislation to control prices, to regulate furnished tenancies and to repeal Mr Heath's Industrial Relations Act was distinctly partisan, but no moves were made to extend nationalisation of industry significantly. The first, hurried budget was mildly progressive in its direct tax changes and increased food subsidies, but some of this assistance to the less well off was cancelled out by the increases in

51

coal and electricity prices.

Particular emphasis was placed on industrial policy. There were proposals to increase centrally planned investment through the National Enterprise Board, for more local industrial planning through the suggested planning agreements with individual firms, for greater financial aid to industry, and for establishing some industrial co-operatives. The blueprint for this intended industrial activity was a White Paper on the regeneration of British industry which set out Labour's broad industrial policy – and which created a major crisis in Whitehall. The initial draft of this Paper was originally written by Ministers and aides in the Department of Industry in very aggressively interventionist language (referred to as 'Bennery' by the rest of Whitehall). The Prime Minister was disturbed by this and asked my Downing Street Policy Unit to rewrite it, which we did in July 1974, much to the annoyance of the Secretary of State for Industry, Tony Benn. We then closeely monitored the progress through Parliament of the Industry Bill, as the Prime Minister was afraid that amendments would be introduced which would restore some of Mr Benn's more extreme initial ideas. We also became involved in the proposed reorganisation of British Leyland. The Ryder Report in early 1975 on which this operation was based seemed to us wildly optimistic. It contained proposals for investing £3 billion over the following seven years with few mechanisms to monitor the efficient use of this money and little prospect of a financial return. Nothing serious was to be done to reduce the ludicrously large range of British Leyland models – BL then had seventy-one passenger models incorporating thirteen different engines in nineteen different sizes, together with three complete ranges of lorries, two of buses and two of juggernauts. This was a far larger programme than that of Volkswagen and Fiat combined, although both were much bigger than BL. Unfortunately, despite efforts made by us and others to impose some rationalisation, little was done until Sir Michael Edwardes was brought in to run the firm properly some years later. Labour's problem was that its general commitment to industrial investment and maintaining full employment, as well as its close ties with the trade unions, made it politically difficult to cut out the bad parts of British industry, even though that was essential for its long-term efficiency and survival.

The humiliating negotiations to rescue Chrysler's automobile operations in the UK in December 1975 (in which I participated as the Prime Minister's personal representative) were an extreme example of this. The American management looked and talked like a Hollywood version of Chicago 'hoods' from the 1930s and they made us offers which they knew we could not refuse. Basically, they wanted the UK Government to pay for their future investment here, with them taking most of the profits if it succeeded but the British Government carrying the first £40 million of losses if it failed. Eric Varley and his prim officials from the Department of Industry were deeply shocked by the blunt way in which Mr Riccardo and his sleek henchmen stated that either we gave them £184 million or they would simply pull out and leave us with the redundancy and unemployment costs. The officials inclined to resist, but Harold Lever and I knew that the Prime Minister wished to settle at almost any price in order to avoid the unemployment and the threat of resignation from his Scottish Ministers. (The latter feared riots at Chrysler's Glasgow Linwood plant, although soon afterwards virtually the whole workforce there offered itself for voluntary redundancy.) Therefore, against our better instincts, we settled; the taxpayer was forced to pay and Chrysler UK survived.

The Cabinet was also faced in 1974 with a tide of impending bankruptcies – Alfred Herbert, Burmah Oil, Ferranti, Aston Martin – not to mention the scandal of the Crown Agents, a domino succession of property collapses, and one of the big four clearing banks reported to No. 10 as being in danger of insolvency. Therefore, after the February election we were occupied primarily with industrial policy together with a string of *ad hoc* crises. Actually, in the absence of a clear macro-economic or counter-inflation strategy, our interventionist industrial proposals were then Labour's most visible economic policy.

The tension over the industrial policy White Paper began a long period of hostility and manoeuvring between the Prime Minister and his Industry Secretary. Partly encouraged by senior civil servants, partly disturbed by the universal animosity expressed by industry towards Mr Benn, but also partly because of his own personal belief that Tony was indeed a danger to political navigation, Mr Wilson decided in the summer of 1974 that he would try to provoke Benn to resign – and anyway would ultimately move him from the Industry post to some less important department (again hoping that this final humiliation would lead to his resignation). I never shared the Prime Minister's optimism on this point. It seemed transparently clear to a detached observer that there was no humiliation which Tony Benn would not swallow in order to stay in the Cabinet. Having the Policy Unit rewrite his White Paper was one of many affronts to which he bravely turned the other cheek over the next five years. Mr Wilson did indeed demote Benn to the Department of Energy a year later, but he accepted that, and neither Mr Wilson nor Mr Callaghan ever carried out their often mentioned threats to grasp the nettle and sack him. Perhaps, in the immortal words of President Lyndon Johnson, each on reflection preferred to have Tony Benn inside the tent urinating out, than outside urinating in.

Actually the struggle over industrial policy in 1974–5 was more than a political power battle. The substantive issues concerning industrial policy were important and the ambitious interventionist policies set out in Labour's 1973 Programme probably began with considerable support inside the new government. Mr Wilson certainly appeared genuinely enthusiastic during the February 1974 election and his personal team then shared that view. However, the united hostility of industry could not be discounted. Based on a long-standing working knowledge of industry, many industrial managers whom we knew to be supporters of the Labour party expressed dismay and made profound and detailed criticisms of the policy proposals. Against this, the speeches made by Tony Benn, and the industrial policy papers from his left-wing advisers and from the research department at Labour party headquarters, appeared distinctly ideological and impractical. Indeed, on meeting these people I found that none of them conveyed the impression that they had any direct experience of working life or had the least idea what made a factory or a service industry succeed or fail. To someone such as myself, the son of a factory worker from the poorest working class, listening to the aristocratic fantasies of Tony

Benn or the middle-class fantasies of Mrs Frances Morrell or Mr Francis Cripps was always entertaining, but it had nothing to do with the realities of industrial life.

This problem became more acute when Labour returned from the disappointing October 1974 election still with barely a parliamentary majority. It is possible to impose a rigid ideological policy when backed by an election mandate and a large parliamentary majority (as Mrs Thatcher demonstrated after 1979). But a minority government has great difficulty in imposing a non-consensus partisan policy, especially in a major policy area. Admittedly this was not perceived as a great difficulty by some comrades and supporters of Mr Benn in the constituency sections of the Labour party, as their adherence to the principles and conventions of parliamentary democracy was at best tenuous. However, for Mr Wilson and most of his Cabinet it set limits to what could be imposed upon the uniformly hostile management of British industry.

The Prime Minister also shrewdly realised that with his fragile parliamentary base he could fight only one major policy battle at a time – and after the summer of 1974 that battle had to be not about academic planning agreements in industry but over the renegotiation of Britain's membership of the EEC. The European issue was bound to split the Cabinet and the party and it therefore required all of Mr Wilson's attention and skill. Industrial policy had to be rewritten, diluted and moved from the centre of the political stage. Tony Benn's army of the left was diverted from the dangerous fields of British industry, whereupon it launched itself with equal passion and innocence upon the deceptively inviting marshes of the EEC. Once committed and trapped there, Mr Benn was blown up by a referendum of the British people. The Prime Minister could then transfer him, impotent to resist and unwilling to resign, to the minor outpost of the Department of Energy. Although the Prime Minister could for a time exalt in his victory over his Cabinet colleague, unfortunately for Mr Wilson (and subsequently Mr Callaghan), the victim, to his credit, never for long admitted defeat. His resilience was remarkable. In those heady days Tony Benn was like a new squash ball: you could stand a piano on him, but when you moved it he bounced back into shape. Through many hours of humiliation from his Prime Minister and criticism and contempt openly expressed by his colleagues in Cabinet, Mr Benn preserved his cool – indeed an almost clinical and disturbingly calm – demeanour and that peculiar and unwavering gleam in his eyes. He saw the impending joyous collapse of social democratic capitalism and confidently awaited his destiny to rebuild a new model Britain. That destiny would clearly be best executed from within rather than without the ruined citadels of power. Therefore any Cabinet seat, even at the Department of Energy, was better than none.

While the Cabinet disposed of industrial policy and renegotiated membership of the EEC, the nation's economic problems were left to simmer on a back burner. Few within Government had a desire or even any incentive to hurry forward the unpromising prospect of coming to grips with the lurking economic horrors. A senior Treasury official told me in the summer of 1974 that the Treasury was not intending to put forward any economic proposals until after the inevitable second general election, when it would introduce a crisis package with statutory control of wages and a prices freeze. I briefed Mr Wilson in the middle of May on the basis of a very worrying paper written by my chief Economic Adviser, Andrew Graham, in which he pointed out that we were on course for hyperinflation, inevitable devaluation and a likely Treasury response that would demand public expenditure cuts and statutory wage controls. Ministers were completely unaware of these gloomy prospects and I suggested that the Prime Minister should confront the Chancellor with these issues as soon as possible in order to determine how they should be handled. However, when Chancellor Healey came to No. 10 in late May to make a rare report to the Prime Minister on economic strategy, he did not emphasise his department's long-term worries. He discussed the need for a second budget in the autumn and pointed out that his proposals for a gift tax and for oil company taxation would lead to a very heavy Finance Bill, and this had to be planned in the context of a likely autumn general election. He was characteristically buoyant, based on the fact that exports and the balance of payments were looking better and the Treasury was forecasting annual growth for the Gross Domestic Product

(GDP) of 4 per cent per annum through to 1979 (a prediction which turned out to be mildly optimistic). Interestingly, he also pointed out that the Treasury wished to see an effective sterling depreciation of around 3 per cent per annum in order to maintain Britain's export competitiveness, given the expected high domestic inflation. The Prime Minister enquired about unemployment prospects, but his mind was on more immediate electoral prospects and this distraction was even more apparent at the beginning of August when, before leaving for my family holiday in France, I briefed the Prime Minister on the need to begin preparing public and ministerial opinion for the inevitable switch towards an incomes policy. By then the October general election date had already been decided upon privately in No. 10.

After the October election (in which the Government secured only a tiny, and brief, majority), Ministers were again diverted from economic issues to other matters. First were the EEC renegotiations, which continued until March 1975 and which were followed by the Paris and the Dublin summit meetings of the European Heads of Government. There was a two-day Cabinet on the EEC on 17–18 March, leading up to the national referendum campaign in May and June 1975; inevitably, the EEC absorbed a great deal of Cabinet's and the Prime Minister's time. It was a very delicate political operation and Harold Wilson was extremely skilful in his handling of a totally divided Cabinet. Originally in 1972 a majority of the Labour party in the country, in Parliament, and of the Prime Minister's senior colleagues were against Britain's joining the EEC. A majority, although not quite as large a majority, were now against remaining in the Community. By skilful management and timing, Mr Wilson finally persuaded sufficient of his Cabinet colleagues to change their minds in order to secure a majority among them to recommend staying in the EEC – and by holding a referendum he diluted the Labour party constituency opposition among a national majority.

Mr Wilson and his Foreign Secretary, James Callaghan, worked in close tandem on the renegotiations concerning British membership of the EEC. These were thrashed out both in detail in constant diplomatic negotiations, and on broad principles at a succession of summit meetings of the European

Heads of Government (all of which I attended). Britain pursued a number of genuine reforms in the workings of the EEC which we believed would be for the Community's benefit as well as ours. The EEC budget required fundamental changes in order to protect the UK from having to pay vast sums to richer neighbours. A number of small improvements were made in the 1974–5 renegotiations (much more was done later by Mrs Thatcher). However, satisfactory reforms depended on radical changes in the Common Agricultural Policy, which we are still awaiting. We also sought guaranteed access to the UK market for Commonwealth products, especially cheap food, and provisions to retain sovereignty by the UK Parliament. Some concessions were extracted and the Prime Minister and the Foreign Secretary were able to make big play with these in order to justify recommending to a sceptical Labour party that Britain remain in the EEC. The key factor was the decision to hold a national referendum – which had originally been pressed for most strongly by Mr Benn and left-wing opponents of the EEC. The referendum was conducted in a unique way, with members of the Labour Cabinet given freedom to support whichever position on the EEC they preferred. Even so, the Government was not neutral. The fact that the Prime Minister and the Foreign Secretary recommended a vote for staying in the EEC carried great weight – especially as Mr Wilson had been a prominent critic of the early entry terms.

The official campaign to remain in the Community was masterminded from the Foreign Office where every morning there was a strategy meeting in the Ambassador's waiting room. James Callaghan or, more often, his junior Minister Roy Hattersley took the chair. Two Labour MPs, John Grant and Bill Price, together with the Foreign Secretary's Press Officer, attended to give advice on media relations. The Chief Whip, Bob Mellish, was also often there and I went as a representative from No. 10. The two leading Foreign Office officials were Michael Butler (later our Ambassador to the EEC) and John Weston, assisted by a specially established Referendum Unit within the Foreign Office. The proceedings usually opened with a report by Bob Worcester of MORI on the latest opinion poll. These polls were specially commissioned for the purpose of the meeting (although not paid for from official sources). Through-out the campaign, the figures showed roughly two-thirds of the electorate to be in favour of staying in the EEC, thus giving Mr Wilson a comfortable victory. Actually I sensed that he was never very sympathetic towards the EEC – or indeed to anywhere abroad except the old Commonwealth. However, he viewed it as a wider issue. To have pulled out of Europe would have put Britain in the hands of the Little Englander isolation-ists who in the Labour party were the Prime Minister's left-wing enemies and in the Conservative party were often the worst kind of right-wing extremists. Mr Wilson was basically a 'main-stream' man and, like Whitehall and much of sensible middle-class England, he was for staying in. When he finally declared his own preference in that direction, it influenced many doub-ters. Even Joe Haines, a long-standing critic of the EEC, finally voted for staying in, because it was preferable to the alternative and would be better for the Labour Government. A decision to pull out would have forced the resignation of many Ministers and would have destroyed the Government.

The proposed devolution of constitutional powers to Scotland and Wales (following the Kilbrandon Commission Report) also occupied an enormous amount of Government time in endless Cabinet Committees. They were among the most boring Cabinet Committees I ever attended, although they were impor-tant as a device to resist the advance of Scottish and Welsh nationalism. These discussions continued through the winter and spring until the big Cabinet debate on devolution at Chequers on 16 June 1975, after which they dragged on for another three years until final failure in the Scottish referendum in 1979.

These two major issues, the EEC and devolution, absorbed most of the Cabinet's time and were the reason for a large number of the official papers going round Whitehall after the October 1974 election. Other major issues were neglected. The Cabinet Office regularly produced what was called the 'Forward Look'. This set out the Government's programme in the weeks ahead, what the issues for discussion were, which had been allocated to which Cabinet Committees, when they were due to meet, who was due to be Chairman. I participated in these

Forward Look meetings in the Cabinet Secretary's room. By June 1975 there was an enormous backlog of business, and especially economic business. which had not yet been considered in Cabinet Committee.

Apart from the pressure of time devoted to the EEC renegotiations and to devolution, there were other, less obvious reasons why the Cabinet delayed in coming to grips with economic problems. Harold Wilson sometimes gave the impression of being reluctant to face the growing economic crisis. He had also shrewdly learned from long and painful previous experience that if a major economic crisis is looming it is politically better to wait until the seriousness of the situation is unmistakably apparent to one's ministerial colleagues; only when it is demonstrably serious will they accept that painful decisions must inescapably be taken. That was certainly also the Treasury officials' view in late 1974 and the early summer of 1975, when they were still biding their time, circulating very little paper on economic policy, and waiting for the crisis to erupt. It was perhaps cynical, but certainly realistic, to assume that politicians deal honestly with a crisis only when there is no alternative and it is impossible to avoid it (a characteristic that most human beings share with politicians). So the Treasury, like the Prime Minister, was sitting in wait for the eruption.

For Harold Wilson and his 1974 Labour Government there was in any case a serious difficulty in coping with the particular kind of economic problems with which they were then faced. The difficulty lay in the fact that the Labour party had fought and won the 1974 elections (especially the one in February) on manifesto commitments which were apparently incompatible with a tough policy against wage inflation. Mr Wilson had made many speeches explaining Labour's priorities, which included the pursuit of full employment, higher economic growth and higher public expenditure. He had also frequently outlined why Labour rejected an incomes policy, at least in the normally understood sense of agreed or imposed limits on pay increases. A statutory incomes policy had been specifically rejected and a good deal of criticism had been directed at Conservative Prime Minister Heath over this question. Therefore it was not an easy situation for Mr Wilson to handle politically; the economic crisis which was looming in 1974–5 was one of inflation, fuelled by pay increases rocketing towards 30 per cent, and of public spending and trading deficits, both of which were alarmingly high, still increasing and forecast to rise beyond the Government's capacity to finance them. They were the kind of problems which traditionally require tough and deflationary remedies, including possibly an incomes policy. Such strategies would clearly breach the very specific election commitments which had been made to the electorate in 1974 and to the trade unions and the Labour party conference many times beforehand.

While the economic situation deteriorated throughout early 1975, with the Treasury sitting in wait and with Ministers diverted on to other issues, we in the Downing Street Policy Unit knew that tough remedies could not be long delayed. The latest Treasury forecasts showed the Public Sector Borrowing Requirement (PSBR) rising to nearly £10 billion, the balance of payments remaining heavily in deficit, inflation (which had already doubled over the previous year) rising towards 30 per cent and unemployment reaching 1 million by the end of 1975. In January Robert Armstrong told me that the Head of the Treasury (Douglas Wass) and the Governor of the Bank of England (Gordon Richardson) had held talks about the looming crisis and concluded that a wage freeze was unavoidable. The Policy Unit at this time submitted a long and gloomy paper to the Prime Minister setting out the harsh realities and choices which faced his Government. We recommended a crisis package including public expenditure cuts to reduce the PSBR, some mixture of import controls or tariffs to help the balance of payments, and a much more vigorous effort to control wage inflation. The Chancellor did bring to Cabinet in mid-March 1975 proposals to cut the planned 1976–7 expenditure by 2 per cent, but the Treasury argument was half-hearted and was not presented as part of a strategy to defeat inflation. It was the usual rag-bag of random cuts in public investment together with the removal of many subsidies (which would actually increase inflation). Defence, as was often the case, simply refused to accept or even discuss half of its proposed cuts, whereas the cuts in Education, the National

Health Service and public industry investment were imposed in full.

It was just a matter of time before the crisis broke. However, it was not surprising that Labour Ministers hesitated before reneging on their election commitments and moving towards an incomes policy, an action which would mean confrontation with the trade unions. It was still only a year since Mr Heath had fought the trade unions. He had been thrown out and Labour had scraped back into office amid much rhetoric about consensus being Labour's strength and confrontation the Tory sin. It was not easy even for a Prime Minister of Mr Wilson's experience to execute this apparent U-turn. The first tentative public step towards a new economic policy was taken in the budget of 1975, which incorporated the already agreed £1 billion of public expenditure cuts with some modest tax increases. The net deflationary effect of the budget was about £1.75 billion and it was the first approach towards grasping the economic realities. Ministers accepted this measure with little reaction. Half of the cuts were in capital investment and were symptomatic of the long-standing problem faced by Conservative and Labour Governments alike; it is always easier to make cuts in investment than in current expenditure (such as staff and salary bills). Many of Britain's current and long-standing economic problems stem from that situation.

The economic crisis finally came to a head in June 1975. In May, Denis Healey had come to Cabinet with a package of a further £3 billion of public expenditure cuts to be spread over 1975–9 in addition to the £1 billion recently agreed in the budget. The Cabinet rejected his proposals, proving that the Treasury had apparently been justified in its previous policy of waiting. It was evident that Cabinet Ministers would still not confront the problem unless they had no alternative. The opposition to the proposed cuts was led from the left by Tony Benn and Barbara Castle, who were against all public expenditure cuts and favoured all public expenditure increases (except in Defence). They were supported by Ministers of every political persuasion from the spending departments, each of whom opposed cuts in his or her own policy area. The latter were for the most part backed intellectually by Anthony Crosland, who was on principle both in favour of all public expenditure and opposed to all conventional Treasury thinking. This motley combination proved too much for the Chancellor – especially as the Prime Minister did not give a strong lead in his defence; indeed, he did not take a firm position either way – and the first proposal for major cuts which would force a crisis was defeated. However, it could only be a matter of time. Simultaneously, Cabinet Ministers weakly approved an increase in pay for railway workers of 30 per cent.

Against this economic background sterling came under pressure. In mid-June 1975 Denis Healey told Cabinet that a crisis package would have to be announced by July as sterling would not hold for much longer. A week later the Prime Minister said to me in a private conversation that 'something must be done' about the way wages were rising and he asked for some suggestions. I held a day-long meeting of the whole Policy Unit to thrash out some proposals. As was often the case, we were joined by the Press Officer, Joe Haines, whose fertile mind and shrewd political judgments were invaluable to us. Together we drew up and submitted to the Prime Minister the first of two substantial papers on incomes policy. This memorandum opened with a stark warning that without a new policy initiative sterling would be down to $1.65 by the end of 1976 (it was then over $2). We therefore suggested that the Government announce a radical economic package. It should contain a pay policy, but voluntary rather than statutory, in order not to conflict totally with previous election pledges. The policy should be based on a £6 per week simple norm increase for everybody, a suggestion that was made by Joe Haines (originally he proposed £5) who argued that to be acceptable an incomes policy should be simple. Everybody would understand what they could buy with £5 or £6. A flat-rate increase also had the attraction over a percentage rise of giving the low paid a bigger percentage increase than the highly paid. I made a further proposal that, although the policy would be voluntary, it should be backed by what I called a 'battery of sanctions'. In other words, any private employer breaking the policy would have tax penalties imposed, as well as being discriminated against in Government contracts, regional subsidies, investment allowances etc. I also said there should be a price code to ensure that prices as well as wages were held down. In the public sector, pay research, comparability and arbitration should be suspended. In the case of local authorities the rate support grant and loan sanction would be used to dissuade the use of higher rates to finance higher wage settlements. We even went so far as to suggest that honours be withheld from the management of firms which went against the norm and that tax rebates for trade unionists who went on strike in pursuit of pay settlements above the norm should be delayed until after the end of the tax year. The heart of the policy's credibility was bound to depend on the support of the TUC. We suggested adding this additional battery of sanctions in order to make the TUC's job easier.

Mr Wilson responded quickly and positively to our policy suggestions. He was attracted because they enabled him to have an effective incomes policy without breaching all past commitments to the electorate and to the Labour movement not to have a *statutory* policy. We had therefore achieved our prime political objective in devising this package.

The Treasury was informed of the Policy Unit's suggestions and immediately opposed them. The Treasury wanted a full statutory policy backed by the criminal law. Over the final two weeks in June there was a savage and very enjoyable Whitehall battle. The Prime Minister summoned a Cabinet at Chequers (which I attended) to discuss pay policy – the first time that pay policy had been considered formally and collectively by Cabinet Ministers. Taking it to Chequers was a symbol that it was a special occasion. This Cabinet decided in principle to have a pay policy; a crucial step for the Prime Minister because the Labour party's public stance was still apparently against the introduction of an incomes policy. However, Cabinet also decided to oppose a statutory policy, so the approach which we had adopted in the Policy Unit papers provided the Government with a way forward.

Following this Cabinet decision in principle, the Whitehall machine was fully switched on to producing a pay policy of some kind. A committee designated PIP (Prices and Incomes Official Committee) was given the task of analysing the options in detail. Meanwhile at ministerial level, pay policy formally came under a standing ministerial Cabinet Committee designated MES (Ministerial Economic Strategy Committee). The Prime Minister also concurrently established a third and secret ministerial Cabinet Committee (MISC 91) to discuss pay policy. There was nothing unusual or deceitful in setting up this secret committee of half a dozen senior colleagues. The Prime Minister knew that he was entering a crisis which could split the Cabinet, or his party, or both, and he did not want to face such a situation alone. If he carried his senior colleagues with him during all the pay discussions, they would be more likely to support him when the issue finally came to the crunch. He did not want to commit himself to an incomes policy and then find his colleagues backing off, leaving him vulnerably exposed in a position which his party would instinctively dislike. Normally this process of discussion would happen openly in regular Cabinet. However, the incomes policy was such a sensitive issue that it could not be exposed too early to all colleagues. The Prime Minister did not want it to become immediately a left-right battle ground, with daily leaks to the *Guardian* of sensitive policy papers. Also, as it was such a delicate political issue and not just a question of economic policy, he wanted to include senior Ministers who were not normally members of the regular ministerial Economic Strategy Committee as well as to exclude some Ministers who were regular members.

Therefore three Cabinet Committees in all – two ministerial and one official – were at work considering the pay issue. The ministerial MISC 91 met on 26 June. The Policy Unit had provided the Prime Minister with another briefing paper the day before and one or two sympathetic Cabinet Ministers had also been shown the document. It set out in more detail our proposal for a voluntary policy backed by sanctions. MISC 91 responded positively and concluded that a credible voluntary policy was what was needed. At the same time the Secretary of State for Employment, Michael Foot, was, with the Prime Minister's knowledge, in constant meetings with the TUC discussing his own preference for a totally voluntary policy.

Consequently three versions of incomes policy were simultaneously under active discussion in late June 1975: Michael Foot's totally voluntary policy, the Policy Unit's modified voluntary policy backed by sanctions, and the Treasury's full-blown statutory policy. I quickly learned from contacts in the Treasury that it had decided to try to get the voluntary proposals rejected and to 'bounce' a statutory policy through Ministers. I spoke to the Prime Minister about this and warned that, unless pressure was put on the Treasury, the voluntary approach would not be given a fair run in Whitehall. He responded positively and immediately despatched to the Treasury what is the most commanding document ever sent in British government – a Prime Minister's minute. This did not reveal explicitly that he knew what the Treasury was up to, but it did give blunt instructions not to proceed further with arguments for a statutory policy and to start analysing and constructing a voluntary policy along the lines already supported in MISC 91. He did not specify a precise pay norm, which was not yet clearly established, although he mentioned a range of 5–10 per cent. However, he made it clear to the Treasury as to the lines on which it should and should not proceed.

The Treasury ignored the Prime Minister's instructions. Instead it submitted to Cabinet at the end of June a paper on pay policy which, while acknowledging the suggestions for a voluntary policy, quickly dismissed them as impractical, and moved on to discuss and recommend only one approach – a full statutory policy.

The economic and Whitehall crisis came to a head on Monday 30 June. On the previous Friday, as the Prime Minister was leaving for Chequers in mid-afternoon, he said to me that he had a feeling that at some point on Monday the Governor of the Bank of England would arrive at Downing Street to tell him there was a terrible sterling crisis. On the Monday morning the Prime Minister went to the Royal Agricultural Show at Stoneleigh in Warwickshire. He returned after lunch and, as he entered through the front door of No. 10, the Governor came through the back door from the Cabinet Office together with the Chancellor of the Exchequer. Other Cabinet Ministers were also assembling at that time in the hallway and corridors of No. 10 for a meeting of the secret MISC 91 to discuss pay policy. They were kept waiting for nearly half an hour while the Prime Minister took the Governor and the Chancellor upstairs to his study. The Governor revealed, as Mr Wilson had earlier forecast, that sterling was indeed collapsing. Apparently £0.5 billion had been lost from the official reserves in the last few days. Against that background, the Prime Minister was urged to support the Chancellor in his proposals for a statutory pay policy. The famous Treasury 'bounce' technique had been launched, with the Bank of England as a powerful ally.

The Governor of the Bank of England left Downing Street, and the Prime Minister and the Chancellor went into the Cabinet room for the MISC 91 meeting. There Denis Healey made his plea to Ministers for a statutory policy. He asked approval for two White Papers: one to be published the very next day would propose a statutory incomes policy with a 10 per cent pay norm; the other, to be produced the following week, listing massive public expenditure cuts and price controls. Mr Healey wanted to give Parliament advance warning of these cuts the following day at the same time as publishing the statutory pay policy, and for both things he needed Cabinet approval.

The assembled Ministers in MISC 91, who anyway did not constitute a full Cabinet, did not explicitly support the Chancellor's proposals. Most just listened solemnly and James Callaghan, the Foreign Secretary, actually appeared to oppose them. He said that he believed in letting sterling float rather than repeatedly bashing the economy in order to defend a particular exchange rate. Mr Callaghan had emerged from his 1964–7 experience as Chancellor scarred in a number of ways. He had become sceptical of the various predictable kinds of Treasury and Whitehall conventional wisdom. This was one of his strengths when he later became Prime Minister. However, sitting in the Cabinet room it was ominously clear to me that Mr Wilson was taking a less robust view. Eight months earlier he had responded to a Policy Unit paper setting out the bleak economic situation ahead by writing on it in longhand: 'I regard any attempt to regulate incomes by statutory means to be out.' Now the situation was clearly reversed. He had been converted by the familiar tolling of the sterling bells and he now believed that it was necessary to introduce a statutory policy.

On the same evening of Monday 30 June, we held a State dinner in No. 10 for Monsieur Tindemans, the Prime Minister of Belgium. Harold Wilson and his wife Mary stood in line at the entrance to the large White Reception Room to greet the guests (who included Michael Edwardes, my friend David Sainsbury, the novelist John Fowles, and several senior trade unionists). Joe Haines and I stood behind the hosts and between handshakes the Prime Minister turned round repeatedly to continue a vigorous argument on incomes policy; we were still putting the voluntary case and he was now arguing for a statutory policy. Understandably enough, he grew irritable and, smiling at each guest in turn, he snapped at us that we were not being sufficiently realistic. It was quite a gruelling evening. Then at midnight, as the dinner guests were departing, the inevitable Treasury memorandum 'bounced' into No. 10. It was a draft of the next day's statement to Parliament by the Chancellor, to be cleared by the Prime Minister immediately and by Cabinet first thing in the morning. The Private Secretaries helpfully showed the document to Joe Haines and me. It contained a totally stark statement of a statutory 10 per cent pay policy, with criminal sanctions. It sounded so familiar that I went down to my office and checked the text against the parliamentary statements made in relation to Mr Heath's earlier incomes policy (which Harold Wilson had so savagely denounced). It actually used many of the same phrases. Officials had apparently taken out of the Treasury pigeon-hole the earlier tried and faithful policy which, as I pointed out to Mr Wilson, may well have been tried, but it had also completely scuppered Mr Heath.

We were well down the statutory incomes policy path again and the Prime Minister was apparently convinced that there was no alternative. Joe Haines and I sat down together in the Press Office and after a depressing discussion we decided to make one last approach to the Prime Minister.* We drafted, signed and sent upstairs a joint minute in which we stated why the Treasury proposal was wrong and that its political implications were incalculably damaging in that it would divide his Cabinet, it would divide his party, it would alienate the trade unions – and then it would be unenforceable. The Prime Minister, having received and read our minute, at first sent a message through a

* Joe Haines's description of this episode can be found in his book *The Politics of Power* (Cape, 1977).

civil servant saying that we were wrong and were becoming 'neurotic' about a statutory incomes policy. There was nothing more to be said, so he went to bed in the flat and we left Downing Street for the night.

However, the Prime Minister telephoned Joe again later to say that he had reflected further and concluded that we were right. He would support the Policy Unit's approach to a voluntary policy. He had already asked for the Chancellor to come to see him first thing in the morning – before the Cabinet meeting which had been arranged to approve formally the White Paper and the parliamentary statement on a statutory incomes policy which the Treasury had sent the night before. True to his word, the Prime Minister told Denis Healey that he had changed his mind and that we were going for a voluntary rather than a statutory policy. The Chancellor (as happened later in 1976 when Mr Callaghan imposed a cuts package far smaller than the Treasury wanted) was commendably agnostic and readily abandoned his officials' proposals. He certainly did not want to be exposed advocating a statutory policy contrary to party policy without the support of his Prime Minister. Mr Wilson and Mr Healey therefore went together into Cabinet to support the voluntary approach, although the papers prepared to go before Ministers were those from the Treasury announcing a statutory policy.

Stage one of the political problem presented by moving towards an incomes policy was thus negotiated and Cabinet Ministers were safely in line. The next stage of the operation was to win round the TUC. On the day following the Cabinet meeting, Jack Jones, the powerful left-wing leader of the giant Transport Workers' Union, was flown to London by private aeroplane. The Prime Minister and the Chancellor met with him and won him round to supporting a pay norm as part of a voluntary policy. Jones suggested a £6 norm instead of Joe Haines's original £5, which was acceptable as a small price to pay for such valuable support. (Jack Jones was also allowed to take credit for inventing the pay policy, although in fact he came fairly late on to the battlefield.) To his credit, Jack Jones quickly converted Hugh Scanlon of the Engineers' Union. With the 'terrible twins' of the union left wing on board, and the calm support of the ever helpful Len Murray, it was possible formally to approach the TUC, which on 3 July accepted the principle of a voluntary policy.

The only remaining institutional difficulty lay with the Treasury, which now had the job of writing and publishing a White Paper advocating a voluntary policy in which its officials did not believe. Although civil servants are usually experienced and impressively skilled at such things, on this occasion the Treasury did not do it very well. When the draft White Paper arrived in Downing Street at the beginning of July, we at the Policy Unit as well as the Downing Street civil service Private Secretaries were deeply disappointed by its language and tone. The underlying scepticism and transparent lack of enthusiasm for the new voluntary policy was likely to leave trade unionists and the whole country as unconvinced as the Treasury mandarins. Therefore, the Policy Unit sat down for some twenty hours of continuous work and drafted an alternative White Paper, which we submitted to the Prime Minister and the Cabinet Secretary that weekend. The then Cabinet Secretary, Sir John Hunt, did not habitually support special advisers against the regular Whitehall machine. On the other hand, he did not always instinctively support the then Permanent Secretary at the Treasury, Sir Douglas Wass, either. On this occasion (and not for the first or last time) he intervened very positively on our behalf and on the Saturday morning telephoned both the Prime Minister and myself to say that he thought the Policy Unit's draft was better than the Treasury's. The Prime Minister agreed and issued instructions that our version was to be used as the basis for the incomes policy White Paper. It was a triumph and a reward especially for Andrew Graham, Gavyn Davies and David Piachaud, the Policy Unit advisers who had worked so hard with me on the details of our alternative paper. It helped greatly to establish the value of the Downing Street Policy Unit in the eyes of the Prime Minister and its credibility in Whitehall. Relations with the Treasury officials henceforward improved dramatically since, as true professionals, they bore no malice but recognised that we were an important part of the Whitehall power game. The Treasury consulted and informed us on most subsequent economic policy proposals, including budgets.

8 Michael Foot, Tony Benn, Peter Shore and Barbara Castle – the anti-Europe group in the Cabinet in 1975.

9 Harold Wilson with his wife Mary (Joe Haines behind) on their way to vote for Europe in the referendum.

10 Denis Healey, Harold Wilson and Michael Foot launch the Social Contract incomes policy in July 1975.

11 Defence Secretary, Roy Mason, with the army in Belfast in August 1975.

12 Robin Butler, Harold Wilson's Private Secretary (and later Mrs Thatcher's Principal Private Secretary), stands behind the Prime Minister, and next to the future Prime Minister.

13 The Cabinet emptying on to the pavement in Downing Street, September 1976.

14-18 The Mandarins:
Above left Victor Rothschild,
Head of Central Policy Review
Staff, 1971-5.
Above Robert Armstrong,
Principal Private Secretary to
Harold Wilson, 1974-5.
Left Sir Douglas Wass,
Permanent Secretary to HM
Treasury, 1974-83.
Below left Sir Kenneth Stowe,
Principal Private Secretary to
Prime Ministers Wilson and
Callaghan.
Below Sir Kenneth Berrill, Head
of the CPRS, 1975-80.

There was still of course much detailed work to be done on the incomes policy, which was argued through endless Cabinet Committee meetings in June and early July. Particularly tricky was the question of whether to support the proposed battery of sanctions with legislative or merely voluntary reserve powers. The accompanying package of £2 billion public expenditure cuts also took a little time to identify. However, on Friday 11 July 1975 Mr Wilson himself unveiled the new pay policy at a big press conference. Because it was a voluntary policy he was able to announce the full support of the trade union movement. He could also for that reason – and with skilful choice of language – claim that it was not quite a U-turn from his and his party's earlier commitments.

The rest of the summer of 1975 was spent hammering out the details, some of which were not without interest. One day I went across to the Treasury for a discussion on the final draft of the White Paper and I noticed that a new brief paragraph had been added which said that 'fees and increments' were excluded from the constraints of the pay norm. When I asked a Treasury friend why we were excluding fees and increments, he replied, waving his hand towards the rest of the room: 'Well, that is them and us.' I asked what he meant. With a guilty grin and pointing to the lawyers who were helping with the drafting, he said: 'They earn the fees and we civil servants earn the increments.' So those making the tough new policy managed to escape some of its rigours.

Overall, Labour's voluntary pay policy was a remarkable success – a fact which has tended to be forgotten during the recent Conservative party and media denigration of incomes policies of all kinds. It was the main factor in dramatically reducing inflation from nearly 30 per cent to single figures during the three years 1975–8 when it operated with TUC support. To many – including some of those trade unionists who foolishly lost faith in it and then violently destroyed it – that incomes policy, however imperfect, must on reflection seem a more humane way of controlling inflation than relying on the deflationary impact of having 4 million unemployed.

The 1975 voluntary incomes policy episode provides some insights into the workings of central government. The first point to be made is that the pay crisis demonstrated that the Whitehall machinery for deciding economic policy was then inadequate. Naturally the Treasury had never encouraged cross-departmental mechanisms to discuss economic policies; like all policy departments, the Treasury preferred to keep its own policy area to itself. There is a centrifugal force operating in Whitehall, tending to take policy-making to individual departments on the periphery; it is against this tendency that the Prime Minister and the Cabinet Office work to centralise decision-making and introduce a collective government view. The Treasury was therefore typical of all departments in wanting to keep others from interfering in what it saw as its own cabbage patch. This attitude was especially prone during an economic crisis, when the Treasury, having secured the last-minute assent of the Prime Minister, traditionally (and usually very effectively) preferred to 'bounce' a crisis package directly through an unprepared Cabinet. Cabinet Ministers usually approved, being frightened by the crisis (especially if it could be said to be damaging the currency), and anyway usually lacking an alternative policy. In July 1975 if we in the Policy Unit had not had the time and the resources to construct our alternative voluntary policy, the Treasury's statutory pay policy would certainly have gone through, mainly because Ministers would not have had a proper chance to examine it beforehand and because they would not have had the time to present any alternative proposals. Furthermore, Jack Jones and Hugh Scanlon would probably have been fighting against rather than for the Labour Government's policy.

The traditional approach of keeping economic policy tight within the Treasury and then 'bouncing' it through Ministers was undermined from 1975 onwards by the existence of special policy advisers who worked to Cabinet Ministers and especially to the Prime Minister. That had been one of Harold Wilson's objectives in 1974 when introducing a more comprehensive system of special advisers into Whitehall, namely to provide alternative economic policy options to those conventionally proposed by the Treasury. The Chancellor and the Treasury of course did not wholly welcome this development, as it made life much more difficult for them if the Prime Minister was receiving alternative and expert economic briefing. I recall having lunch in 1975 with a former Chancellor under Harold Macmillan, Derek Heathcoat-Amory, who said to me, 'I am pleased that you did not exist when I was at the Treasury. It was difficult enough anyway, but at least I knew that when I put something to the Prime Minister he usually accepted it (although this was not always the case, even then, as his predecessor Peter Thorneycroft had discovered). I certainly would not have wanted people like you crawling all over my proposals.' This was a natural Treasury reaction, but it showed the importance of the Whitehall reform to introduce policy advisers into No. 10, a practice which Mr Callaghan and Mrs Thatcher wisely continued. When a Prime Minister and other Cabinet Ministers have economic policy advisers they have alternative economic options. This may unfortunately slow down the process of economic discussion in government, but it hopefully produces more open and better considered economic decisions; it certainly gives the Prime Minister and the Cabinet more power. It means that the Prime Minister can meet the Chancellor having been fully briefed, as we always briefed both Mr Wilson and Mr Callaghan, and having closely scrutinised the Treasury figures, thus enabling the Prime Minister to support the strengths in the Treasury argument, but also to point out the weaknesses, the omissions and, above all, other alternative policy responses. As the Prime Minister became more involved in the details of economic policy and presented such arguments in Cabinet, so other Ministers also played a larger part. The annual budget remained relatively sacrosanct, but even that was subject to more ministerial scrutiny in prior discussions of the overall fiscal balance and public expenditure implications, if not of precise and sensitive tax changes. (Certainly I always knew the detailed contents of all budgets well in advance.) This extension of ministerial and especially prime ministerial involvement in the conduct of economic policy was good for the government of Britain not because the Treasury is or was incompetent; indeed, it is a very impressive body of highly intelligent and dedicated civil servants and it is the most impressive single institution with (and against) which I have worked. However, it inevitably has a limited vision, with traces of Gladstonian candle ends still in its thought processes. It follows that policy dimensions other than simply the Treasury view (or views) need to be introduced into Cabinet discussion.

In this context it should be made clear that the Treasury Ministers themselves contributed greatly to discussion being more open. Denis Healey sportingly and sensibly abandoned the Treasury's statutory proposal in 1975 and advocated the new voluntary policy with skill, conviction and great success. The moment he saw that the TUC was willing to support our voluntary option he seized upon the advantages. Subsequently on other issues he usually placed the economic options fairly and squarely before Ministers. Actually his job was virtually impossible as a lone Treasury voice advocating restraint to a Cabinet packed with Ministers intent on spending. I discussed this question, which had long exercised the Treasury, of its under-representation in Cabinet with the Chancellor and the Prime Minister in 1976 and in due course a second Treasury Minister, the Financial Secretary, was admitted to full Cabinet membership. Joel Barnett performed this role splendidly.

A further characteristic of the Wilson Cabinet was the number of senior figures able to speak with weight and experience on economic matters, a fact which could be helpful if they supported the Chancellor but was intimidating when they were in opposition. Apart from the Prime Minister, there were in Mr Wilson's Cabinet two ex-Chancellors of the Exchequer in James Callaghan and Roy Jenkins. The latter was potentially very influential but in fact did not speak very often, seeming not unjustifiably to be awaiting the unfolding of some scenario of nemesis. Mr Callaghan, then Foreign Secretary, worked very closely with the Prime Minister, discussing policies in advance and usually adding his considerable weight to support the Prime Minister in Cabinet. The Chancellor knew that with the backing of the Prime Minister and the Foreign Secretary he would normally carry the day, and without their support he would certainly lose. He actually had more trouble with two other highly intellectual and entertaining members of the Cabinet, Anthony Crosland and Harold Lever. Each took a delight in exposing the inevitable occasional weaknesses in the Chancellor's argument. Each was fundamentally committed to economic

expansion and against conventional Treasury 'stop-go' policies.
To them the oil shock of 1973–4 was a terrible blow because it
made a degree of deflation unavoidable, even respectable, and
brought an end to the 'party' of endless public expenditure
increases. However, they were a formidable intellectual combination when, usually with devastating wit and humour, they
exposed the alleged 'dreariness' of the orthodox Treasury
approach. Fortunately for the Chancellor, neither had a strong
political base and for as long as he had the Prime Minister with
him, and other Ministers knew that something had to be done
about inflation, Denis Healey was able to resist the Crosland-
Lever arrows with his own impressive armour of strong intellect,
a robust humour and a remarkably thick skin. He had even less
difficulty in dealing with the conventional left wing. Tony Benn,
who could be more brilliant in Cabinet argument than most of
his outside detractors would imagine, actually put up little
opposition over the 1975 pay policy, seeming content (in curious
alliance with Roy Jenkins on this if on nothing else) to be present
to witness and record the final collapse of Wilsonian 'Labour-
ism'. He clearly operated under the bizarre assumption that the
extreme left and not Mrs Thatcher would benefit from that
demise. The left was further weakened by the defection of
Michael Foot, who for a time sincerely pursued the option of a
totally voluntary pay policy operated by the trade unions and
then loyally supported the Government when it took a slightly
different course. He was to become increasingly important, first
to Mr Wilson and later to Mr Callaghan, in holding the
Government and the TUC together under the elastic bonds
of the social contract. For without the support of the TUC
the Labour Government would have foundered – as indeed
happened when it lost trade union support in 1978–9.

A further governmental aspect of the incomes policy discussions in 1975 was that they revealed the inefficiency of the
existing Cabinet Committee machinery. The standing ministerial Economic Strategy Cabinet Committee (MES) met only
rarely while the economic clouds gathered in the first year after
Labour took office. Even then, MES did not seriously discuss
the central inflation problem – or indeed the problem of
unemployment which, although it had doubled during the first

year of this Labour Government, was actually never once on the Cabinet agenda until I primed a senior Cabinet Minister to ask for it to be placed there early in 1975. This certainly was curious to a concerned observer. The MES agenda usually contained such items as oil and exports, which were very important in themselves but were none the less at the margin of the immediate inflation problem. The central economic issues were never discussed in any sustained and systematic way.

Meanwhile, the Prices and Incomes Official Committee (PIO) just passively watched the slide into inflationary crisis. There was little co-ordination of the three relevant committees (MES, PIO and MISC 91) and I could see no logic or coherence in the allocation of items to one agenda or another. Particular pay claims might be discussed in any of the three committees. Different pay aspects of the same industry, affecting different parts of what was basically the same work-force, were discussed at separate committees without any attempt to relate one to another. Moreover, there was little discussion of the relationship of individual pay claims and settlements to the overall inflation outlook.

What was needed (and was subsequently introduced) was to establish a single strategic economic Cabinet Committee which would cover the whole broad economic field and would be serviced by various committees concentrating on particular micro areas of policy. The Cabinet Secretary, Sir John Hunt, finally took this matter in hand, and by the time Mr Callaghan became Prime Minister the machinery for the discussion of economic policy had been much improved.

One further reason for the economic policy vacuum which was evident during the first year of Harold Wilson's 1974 administration was that the Treasury was clearly demoralised following the collapse of Mr Heath's incomes policy. The Treasury gave the impression of having run out of policy ideas and was certainly lacking in self-confidence. It was then interesting to observe how other policy advisory bodies in Whitehall moved willingly into the vacuum. In Whitehall, if one institution is not doing its job properly, ultimately another body moves in. The Cabinet Office under its ambitious Secretary, Sir John Hunt, was at that time the main instigator. Sir John appeared not over impressed by the way the Treasury was being run and he directed his attentions increasingly towards the economic policy field. It was not the first time that the Cabinet Office had taken a high economic profile: it had housed the Economic Section of the Cabinet during and after the Second World War. Although throughout much of its history the Cabinet Office has been primarily concerned with co-ordinating Whitehall and so keeping the wheels of government running, under Hunt it became increasingly involved in policy roles. This happened during the pay policy crisis, and at the same time the Cabinet Office secured dominion over the Treasury in relation to co-ordinating public expenditure cuts. The Central Policy Review Staff (a body of some two dozen policy analysts established in the Cabinet office by Mr Heath and wrongly abolished by Mrs Thatcher) often assisted the Cabinet Secretary in this policy role. It gave him considerable influence over the CPRS policy papers submitted to Cabinet from his office – although curiously the CPRS played a very small part in the 1974–5 wage inflation crisis, possibly because this was so political in nature. Such overt Whitehall imperialism led the Cabinet Office at this time into several battles with the Treasury, which the Cabinet Secretary, having easier access to the Prime Minister and more carnivorous instincts than his Treasury opposite number, tended to win.

For the Downing Street Policy Unit, the pay policy debate of 1975 was crucial. We were able to demonstrate to Whitehall both that we had something to contribute and that the Prime Minister listened to our recommendations. From that time also I began verbally briefing some other Cabinet Ministers when they showed interest and even sometimes at their request. This ensured that a wider range of policy options were available to Cabinet. The Policy Unit also began to work much more closely with the Treasury, where the emergence of a new Treasury generation, including Peter Myddleton, Leo Pliatzky, Geoffrey Littler, Gordon Downey and Anthony Rawlinson, made this transformation easier and certainly congenial.

The final significance of the 1975 pay crisis was that it brought Prime Minister Wilson, however reluctantly, back into the centre stage of economic policy-making, because ultimately it was his policy. Details may have originated from his advisers, but constitutionally and politically the Prime Minister's aides are indistinguishable from him. Mr Wilson himself took the vital strategic decision between the options of a voluntary or a statutory policy. He made the right choice and he subsequently guided the policy to success. Through this major policy intervention the Prime Minister converted his 'dignified' role as a Treasury overlord into an effective policy role. Mr Callaghan was to continue the trend, as is seen in the following chapter. Throughout the rest of the Labour Government until 1979, economic policy was on broad strategic issues under the active control of the Prime Minister, although always in very close consultation with his Chancellor. Routine matters of day-to-day economic management lay properly with the Treasury in Great George Street but on the major questions of economic strategy the Prime Minister was very effectively the First Lord of the Treasury in No. 10 Downing Street.

4

The IMF Crisis, 1976

The second policy change made by the 1974–9 Labour Government – and one which definitely constituted a U-turn – was adopting a tougher monetary policy, with big public expenditure cuts and higher unemployment being an inescapable price of that policy. This process of change was interesting not just in policy terms but also because of its intellectual background. Much of what one does in government has no explicit reference to ideas. This, however, was a case where ideas did matter because a sea-change was taking place in economic thinking as Labour took office, and this was partly due to the erosion of Keynesian faith which took place rapidly and was very important. The Labour Governments of the 1940s, the 1960s, and ours in the 1970s, were basically 'Keynesian' in so far as they had economic concepts in their minds and an economic structure in their way of thinking. This was perhaps ironical in view of the fact that J.M. Keynes was in many respects a right-wing Liberal. However, this generation of Labour politicians grew up with a prime attachment to Keynes's commitment to, and economic techniques for securing, full employment. Most of them had never been Marxist in any meaningful systematic sense; they simply held a crude and general kind of Keynesianism at the back of their political minds. I do not suppose many of them had ever read Keynes's *General Theory* (although Anthony Crosland certainly had, and Denis Healey had apparently read virtually everything), but they had absorbed the broad Keynesian approach during a lifetime of political debate and they therefore came into government carrying the Keynesian luggage. However, general faith in that approach was actually being eroded day by day in the mid-1970s. It was being undermined intellec-

79

tually by the critical debate taking place in the universities and the media and by the great publicity given to the advocates of monetarism. It was eroded politically because Labour Governments in the 1970s found they had experienced the disadvantages of the Keynesian approach without enjoying the advantages. Labour pursued the Keynesian priorities of growth, public expenditure and full employment. It was accepted that this might inevitably lead to disadvantages in terms of slightly higher inflation and taxation than might otherwise be the case. In practice we suffered the inflation and the taxation but did not enjoy the growth or the full employment. The same was true of public expenditure. Democratic socialists accept the need for, indeed the virtue of, high public expenditure because of the priority given to better public services, but Ministers during 1974–9 found that they were spending more on public expenditure and not receiving better public services in return. Put simply, Labour was paying for Keynesianism without reaping the assumed benefits. This naturally created political disenchantment.

Of course not every Cabinet Minister was acutely aware of the political erosion of Keynesianism and the intellectual advance of monetarism. Fred Peart, Roy Mason and Stan Orme presumably did not spend many hours of their working days worrying about it because they had more practical things to do. However, the changing intellectual climate in economics mattered greatly and the strong campaign by the Friedmanite monetarists definitely added force and conviction to the Thatcherite critique of Labour and also began to capture the intellectual power centres of decision-making. The pressure had its effects in different ways. For example, although Whitehall never fully believed in the whole monetarist mumbo-jumbo or even that there was a precise mathematical link between growth in money stock and future inflation levels, there was a realisation that Keynesianism simply was not working. There was a recognition that with high public expenditure we did not necessarily ensure good public services, but we certainly suffered from high taxes and high interest rates. It was also clear that a lax monetary stance probably resulted ultimately in higher inflation even if there was not any strictly calculable timing on the cause and effect links between the two. Any such higher inflation probably resulted in higher unemployment and certainly imposed a bigger burden on the poor, who are least able to adjust to inflationary distortions. Indeed, one of the more depressing aspects of working in these Labour Governments was to observe that the left wing, who opposed most specific measures to control inflation, seemed to believe that inflation did not matter and failed to perceive that one of inflation's most damaging consequences is to hurt the poor, involving as it does an automatic redistribution of wealth primarily weighted against the least well-off (the rich can manipulate their wealth into inflation-linked assets). Therefore, as far as I am concerned, inflation is the enemy of a democratic socialist society.

As Keynesianism lost favour, the advantages to the Labour Government of a judicious and pragmatic use of stricter monetarist policies became more apparent. In particular, a more vigorous monetary policy promised to reinforce the anti-inflationary success of the existing incomes policy. For this reason the changes on incomes policy and on monetary policy were closely linked. The IMF crisis which is described below made this policy change more explicit in public – particularly through the later publication by the Treasury of official monetary targets – but actually it merely confirmed and extended a trend already established before 1976.

As far as the individual decision-makers and the institutions in government were concerned, the degree of commitment to the new economic approach varied. Mr Wilson was a trained economist but he seemed to have lost interest in contemporary developments in economic thinking before the debate on monetarism emerged. However, as early as May 1974 the Policy Unit sent the Prime Minister a paper alerting him to the need to deal with the monetarist question and suggesting that he set up a mixed Cabinet Committee of Ministers and officials to consider monetary matters. Mr Wilson did not respond positively. However, over a year later, in December 1975, I submitted to him a long thirty-page paper explaining why monetary policy had become much more central to economic strategy than hitherto. My paper also set out the direct implications of monetarism for various areas of government policy – such as housing, industry and counter-inflation – and concluded that it would be dangerous to leave monetary questions to unilateral decisions made by the Chancellor and the Treasury. We at the Policy Unit were actually saying that the Prime Minister should become more involved in questions of interest rates and exchange rates or he would find that his Government's scope for achievement in other important policy areas would be automatically constrained. There was not much time for Mr Wilson to react to this attempt to persuade Downing Street to play a greater part in the debate (he resigned three months later) but he asked for the paper to be circulated to the Chancellor (although not to the Governor) and then to a restricted group of Ministers for discussion. Mr Wilson's successor certainly followed this line, including establishing the 'economic seminar' in No. 10 to discuss monetary issues. Mr Callaghan as Prime Minister was not and never would be a doctrinal monetarist, but he was instinctively conservative on economic matters and he believed that the main priority of his Government was to defeat inflation, his basic position being that monetary laxity was nearly always wrong. His big speech to the Labour Party Conference at Blackpool in 1976 was the first overt monetarist statement by a senior Labour politician, but it was in fact part of a long process of economic thought and in no way an aberration on the part of Mr Callaghan. He said: 'We have lived for too long on borrowed time, borrowed money . . . there is nothing particularly unsocialist about admitting that it [deficit spending] is no longer, if it ever was, an effective way of maintaining high employment in anything but the very short term . . . We used to think that you could just spend your way out of a recession to increase employment by cutting taxes and boosting government spending. I tell you in all candour that that option no longer exists and that in so far as it ever did exist it worked by injecting inflation into the economy.' Some of the original draft words may have been written by his son-in-law, Peter Jay, but the sentiments, the final phrasing and the tremendous courage and conviction with which they were delivered to an initially unsympathetic Labour Conference audience, were authentic Jim Callaghan.

A pragmatist at heart, the Chancellor Denis Healey was neither a complete Keynesian nor a monetarist, but a Healeyite.

He brought an impressive muscular intelligence to economic affairs and was unlikely to be brainwashed by mumbo-jumbo of any kind. He was also psychologically a 'toughie' and a realist and therefore his instincts were against laxity and for taking a tough stance when necessary. Mr Healey's Treasury officials were very mixed in their views, although all of them were rightly opposed to allowing hyper-inflation. At the top there were some unreconstructed Keynesians who perhaps seemed a bit sloppy intellectually in the new rigorous economic climate, but in the lower ranks were many of a tougher fibre who had absorbed the more sensible contributions of the new monetarist climate.

The Bank of England, which played an extremely important role throughout the IMF episode, contained an equally mixed bag of individual economic attitudes. In some ways the Bank was the reverse of the Treasury, headed as it was by an impressive Governor, Gordon Richardson, who was almost obsessively devoted to defeating inflation. To him this was a moral crusade, to be pursued relentlessly and almost regardless of the cost in terms of higher interest rates and higher unemployment – from which Bank employees, with their subsidised mortgages and job security, were happily immune. However, his attitude was offset by those of his advisers, especially the economists, who were more traditionally Keynesian.

These various strands of thought on monetary policy running through the decision-making institutions of government became of immediate relevance in 1976 when the looming crisis was essentially monetary. Whereas the first strand of Labour's economic crisis concerned the pay explosion in 1975, the second strand in 1976 involved the dramatically worsening public sector deficit and external balance of payments deficit. It culminated as Mr Callaghan came to power and enabled him (as Mr Wilson was enabled over incomes policy) by the opportunity of great events to impose the Prime Minister's inherent authority over the Treasury. In each case economic policy was ultimately conducted from Downing Street.

The situation which Mr Callaghan inherited in April 1976 was very serious. Nine months earlier in August 1975 a special Cabinet had been summoned at Chequers to discuss public expenditure priorities in view of the inevitable package of cuts expected before long. In the autumn the Treasury had produced the regular National Income Forecast (NIF) which showed the Public Sector Borrowing Requirement for 1975–6 rising from £9 billion to £12 billion, which at around 5 per cent of Gross Domestic Product was alarmingly high. The external deficit was forecast to be over £1 billion and rising. Prime Minister Wilson immediately summoned the same secret inner group MISC 91 who had met earlier in the summer to discuss pay policy. At the meeting Chancellor Denis Healey presented three options. Unless Ministers significantly cut public expenditure the alternatives facing the Government were either to introduce import controls (this was floated mainly to frighten Ministers); to devalue sterling by 7 per cent (to frighten the Prime Minister); or to apply to the IMF for a major loan (revealing how early on, still under Harold Wilson's premiership, an application to the IMF was on the agenda). The Ministers did not reach any precise decision at this meeting; they merely discussed the looming crisis in general terms. However, they did indicate that of the three options they preferred the IMF loan – and this was more than a year before it finally happened. Mr Callaghan himself said: 'Let us do the tough things now and get them out of the way.'

For the remainder of the autumn and winter of 1975 the Cabinet was occupied in discussing the public sector cuts which the Treasury proposed for the annual review of public expenditure. The Chancellor initially suggested a reduction of just under £4 billion to be spread over the remaining years of this Parliament, 1976–9. Already the Government was being forced to adopt a stricter economic stance by cutting public expenditure and this meant abandoning some of its policy commitments in the public services. Anthony Crosland, supported by Harold Lever, now began to lead the resistance to this restrictive economic approach, arguing strongly that there was no convincing case for cuts according to the 'resources' theory put forward by the Chancellor. The Treasury was using old-fashioned arguments for expenditure cuts based upon fears of 'overheating'; officials reasoned that it was necessary to squeeze the economy to create what they called 'a hole for expansion'. This was presumably a re-writing of various crisis package documents from the 1940s, 1950s and 1960s, many of which Mr Wilson at least had read at the time. Sadly – as Tony Crosland, supported by others close to the Prime Minister pointed out – there was not the least danger in this new recessionary world of the mid-1970s of any economic overheating, so there was no need to create a hole. Indeed, a bigger hole of under-utilised resources was growing naturally in the British economy every month. In this way the Treasury's tattered old 'resources' argument was successfully knocked down and in the end most participants agreed that the real debate was about confidence in the currency and the unsustainable expansion of the public sector.

The Treasury finally secured Cabinet approval for cuts of about £3.5 billion in January 1976; so the squeeze was already on before James Callaghan took office. This exercise was actually quite a triumph for Chancellor Denis Healey, who for perhaps the first time since 1974 displayed his true calibre, showing great stamina and powers of sustained argument as he guided these measures through a sceptical Cabinet over two long months of wrangling. The authority and credibility of the Treasury, which had been undermined before by the defeat of Mr Heath's policy and by its activities and inactivities over pay policy in 1974–5, were reasserted again. However, it suffered another setback almost immediately.

No sooner had the expenditure cuts been approved early in 1976 than the Treasury decided to secure a fall in the pound in order to make sterling more competitive. However, the Bank of England mishandled the technical attempt to ensure a 'smooth downward adjustment' in the currency and instead precipitated a crisis of confidence which put sterling into free-fall. When other bankers spotted England's central bank selling its own currency they decided to follow the Bank's lead. Sterling slumped and the resulting currency crisis continued through February and March. The pound plunged from $2 to $1.90 on 10 March 1975 and The Bank of England was authorised to spend up to $500 million a day to keep sterling above that level. However, the Treasury was still seeking currency competitiveness: it did not want the rate above $1.95 and in the medium term hoped it would settle around $1.88.

This concept of the smooth downward adjustment of the currency to which the Treasury and the Bank were so attached was never supported in the Policy Unit. It was not clear whether it is better for a currency to fall smoothly, jaggedly, or, as we wanted, in one quick move (the Policy Unit recommended a one-step devaluation followed by strong official support). What is clear is that it is foolish to precipitate a currency slide which is seen by the markets and cannot be controlled.

The last weeks of Harold Wilson's administration were blighted by this sterling crisis (as had been his accession to the Premiership twelve years earlier). Nearly a third of Britain's official reserves were spent in March and April 1976 in order to support the sagging currency. The Prime Minister was understandably angry with the Treasury because of what he saw as an amateurish technical mishandling of the attempted devaluation. Mr Wilson was also upset because he knew (Joe Haines and I had been aware of the precise plans for nearly a year, but admittedly the Chancellor and the Treasury did not know) that he planned to resign as Prime Minister when he reached the age of sixty in March and the last thing he wanted was to step down in the middle of a sterling crisis. In fact, he contemplated delaying his resignation because of it (and his secretary, Lady Falkender, used that as one of several arguments for him to delay). However, fortunately for Mr Wilson the situation stabilised and he was able to resign with dignity and stunning surprise.

Many rumours circulated about the reasons for his resignation. Because it caught people unawares – especially the media – it was alleged to be a sudden move in order to avoid an impending scandal. In fact, when I joined Mr Wilson's Downing Street team in March 1974 he told me to arrange for two years' leave from the London School of Economics because he would retire in the spring of 1976 on reaching his sixtieth birthday. Mr Wilson had often dropped Ministers from the Cabinet when they passed the age of sixty; he seemed to have a fear of garrulous old age and had always shown commendable support for rising young talent. Undoubtedly he was bored with government, having seen it all before and he was fed up with managing the squabbles within the Labour party, where many on the left wing seemed more interested in attacking the Labour leadership than in resisting the return of a Conservative Government. He had also grown tired of the bickering and recurrent hysteria within his own 'kitchen cabinet'. It is also said that his wife, Mary, wished him to retire, although I have no direct evidence of that. There were, of course, the inevitable rumours of scandals, as is so often the case in politics. Odd people, with a lot of money but few socialist credentials, made approaches through the political side and some of these appeared in Mr Wilson's curious resignation honours list.* Some were fortunately removed from the list at the last moment following advice from the Home Office and the Inland Revenue. However, I do not believe this was anything to do with Mr Wilson's resignation. He barely knew some of the less respectable names on his honours list and his departure had been planned for a long time. He had discussed the details with Kenneth Stowe (his Principal Private Secretary) and Joe Haines over the summer of 1975 and the latter had a detailed resignation timetable, which I saw in his personal safe. At first Mr Wilson had thought of resigning in September 1975, and then at Christmas, but he reverted to his original target of Easter 1976, believing that his sixtieth birthday would be a fitting time to step down. His plans were disrupted by first the currency crisis and then by the announcement of Princess Margaret's divorce. Despite the setbacks, he kept basically on course and to his timetable. The whole episode was a triumph of secrecy and discretion for his personal team. When on 16 March 1975 Mr Wilson drove to the Palace to inform Her Majesty The Queen of his intended resignation there was nobody outside No. 10 to witness this beginning of the end of a remarkable prime ministerial career which had covered eight of the last twelve years of British history.

Although the currency crisis had been held in abeyance, Mr Wilson's successor, Mr Callaghan, nevertheless inherited a delicate economic situation. The incomes policy was progressing satisfactorily, with lower pay settlements keeping in line with the agreed £6 norm increases. Some public expenditure cuts had already been approved but more would certainly be

* This episode is described more fully in Joe Haines's *The Politics of Power*.

needed: in the new Prime Minister's first month in Downing Street the contingency reserve for the whole year (the large slice of revenue which the Treasury sets aside to meet unforeseen expenditure contingencies during the financial year) was allocated to various spending programmes. Within three weeks of taking office, the Policy Unit warned Mr Callaghan that a sterling crisis was highly likely and that if the next pay round settled at above 5 per cent he would almost certainly have to go to the IMF for a loan and accept the painful conditions such a move would entail. Sterling was already again under occasional pressure, falling seven cents to $1·70 during the first few days of June. It was therefore no surprise when early in June 1976 the Treasury and the Bank of England told us that in order to reduce the PSBR from £12 to £10 billion another big package of immediate cuts was necessary, otherwise sterling could not be held. The Prime Minister initially resisted this approach and told the Treasury to go first to the IMF for a stand-by credit facility of £5 billion. We therefore received assistance from the IMF well before the major crisis broke. However, although Mr Callaghan had outwardly resisted the Treasury package of cuts, he privately said to me 'We have to do it. We must have an emergency budget. We will have to have more cuts and we had better get it over with soon.'

From that moment in the summer of 1976 Mr Callaghan effectively took over the conduct of the Government's economic policy. His methods were quite different from those of Harold Wilson. For one thing, he was more open with Cabinet colleagues, putting the economic problems starkly before them and encouraging full discussion. Mr Wilson had seemed nervous about full Cabinet discussions, fearing that leaks to the press from rival factions would create problems within the Labour party. He was in some ways a natural Treasury man, skilfully slipping items through Cabinet. Mr Callaghan, on the other hand, sought to carry his whole Cabinet with him all the way, hoping to satisfy – even exhaust – colleagues with discussion and to leave no dissenting Minister (as Mrs Thatcher did to Michael Heseltine in 1986) feeling so angry at the fact that discussion was being stifled that resignation was the only way to voice a particular point of view. Mr Callaghan's approach was to keep his political base wide by embracing everybody in the political debate, while himself giving a clear lead. Mrs Thatcher apparently preferred to define her political boundaries narrowly and to treat all who were unable to squeeze within them as aliens. Mr Wilson opted to leave the question of boundaries blurred and hoped that people would not make too much fuss.

Mr Callaghan personally authorised the Chancellor to lay down his proposals for further public expenditure cuts, telling Denis Healey that he 'must bring them to Cabinet and win the support of Ministers'. (The Treasury also wanted, although it did not yet reveal this, an extra £1 billion of tax revenue.) The Prime Minister then summoned his advisers to Chequers for a crisis summit meeting at which the Chancellor, the top Treasury officials, the Governor of the Bank of England, the Cabinet Secretary, the Prime Minister's Principal Private Secretary (Kenneth Stowe) and myself were present. Mr Callaghan promised his full support in Cabinet for the coming package of expenditure cuts and he specifically asked the Governor: 'Will £1 billion off the expenditure target for this year be enough to hold the currency? If not, let us not duck it, let us face it, do more, and get it over with as soon as possible.' Gordon Richardson assured him that with £1 billion of cuts everything should be all right, although nobody of course can guarantee the behaviour of currency.

The Chancellor put his cuts package before a series of seven Cabinets stretching over two weeks during July 1976. In fact, by then the Chancellor had to announce that he now needed £2 billion of cuts or extra revenue, because the Treasury's original target of spending for the year had already been overspent by a billion. These Cabinet discussions were impressive and fascinating. The Cabinet was basically (but not bitterly) divided into four camps. One stronghold was the small group of Treasury men – Denis Healey and the Financial Secretary Joel Barnett (who was not yet a full member of Cabinet but attended all of these meetings), together with Edmund Dell, an able ex-Treasury Minister who had the instincts and pessimistic character of a natural Treasury man, and the Prime Minister himself who was committed to support Mr Healey. This loyal group was essential for the success of the Chancellor, whose position is inevitably a very lonely one when proposing unpopular policies.

The second group comprised what could be called the 'Keynesian dissenters' who were led by Anthony Crosland. Harold Lever also gave invaluable support to Crosland because he was not only clever but actually understood practical market finance – a fact which gave him a great, almost unique, advantage over the rest of the Cabinet, Whitehall and especially the Treasury. Supporting Crosland and Lever were Roy Hattersley and Shirley Williams who shared the view that there was no case for cuts on the grounds of resources; they also held the assumption that full employment was both desirable and attainable and for this more rather than less public expenditure was required.

Advocating the left-wing 'alternative strategy' was a third group led by Tony Benn, and supported by Michael Foot, John Silkin and Stan Orme from the left, together with Peter Shore, an endearing and independent-minded maverick from the right. They argued for a fundamentally different economic strategy based upon the concept of a 'fortress Britain' allegedly able through import controls, import deposits and currency controls to sustain a high level of public expenditure and employment. Benn also proposed higher taxes on petrol, alcohol and tobacco.

These three groups maintained a high level of usually friendly debate throughout the Cabinet discussions. Sitting more silently around the Cabinet table was a fourth group of Ministers whom any eighteenth-century historian would recognise as a 'King's party'.* Most of them owed their positions in the Cabinet mainly to the personal favour of the Prime Minister, although the best of them, such as Fred Mulley, were valuable and worthy members of any Labour Cabinet. The Prime Minister expected them to follow his lead, and they recognised that in the end they would do so. They were the core of support which the Prime Minister could deliver to his Chancellor in favour of the cuts package. This he ultimately did – although of course along the way they were able and very willing on an individual basis to

* See numerous studies by the Namier school of eighteenth-century historians, including my own *British Politics and the American Revolution* (Macmillan, 1964).

oppose any particular cuts in their own areas of departmental responsibility.

Mr Callaghan's management of this economic debate in July presaged his achievement during the bigger crisis four months later and was superior to anything I had observed earlier. Previously, as was shown in the discussion of pay policy in the last chapter, the Treasury had preferred to wait furtively until the last moment when economic crisis broke, at which point it would 'bounce' through tough measures, hoping that shell-shocked Ministers would approve, or not even realise what was happening. On this occasion, however, the Treasury was compelled to refine its arguments and did indeed eventually make them much more convincing. The left-wing was given every opportunity to raise its alternative strategy of import controls and higher public expenditure, a policy which was to be developed more fully during the later IMF crisis. The Prime Minister once turned to me after one of those long Cabinet meetings and said, 'Ministers have discussed the cuts so often, they come to think they have agreed them.' It was a good tactic, taking the arguments round the table again and again. Apart from anything else, it educated Ministers about the economic realities and prepared them for the even worse news which lay ahead. In contrast to the later, more authoritarian style of Mrs Thatcher, Mr Callaghan also had frequent private meetings with Ministers who seemed troubled, which was another example of good prime ministerial management and it took time and patience on the Premier's part. However, it enabled Mr Callaghan successfully to carry Cabinet Ministers with him and it avoided the succession of resignations which littered the more autocratic career of his successor.

The discussions concluded with two Cabinet meetings on the same day at the end of July when Ministers finally approved £1 billion of cuts from planned public expenditure in 1977–8. The Chancellor thanked his colleagues and then promptly put on the table a second proposal – for £1 billion of National Insurance surcharge. This promised to bring the PSBR down to £10 billion, although at a social cost of 200,000 extra unemployed. The measure was approved and, with the target of £2 billion of expenditure cuts and extra revenues achieved and also believing

that the crisis had been headed off, I went off on my annual
August holiday in France. Meanwhile, always careful to main-
tain his international network in case he needed their help, the
Prime Minister had telephoned Chancellor Schmidt, President
Giscard and President Ford to inform them of what he had
done.

Mr Callaghan experienced a final difficulty with his Energy
Minister, Tony Benn. I was present in the Prime Minister's
study after the final Cabinet agreement when Tony telephoned
to say that he had a problem. He explained that he must consult
with his constituency activists over whether he should now
resign completely from the Cabinet or merely continue to
campaign in public against the Cabinet's decision on cuts in
public expenditure. The Prime Minister replied, 'Tony, why
don't you make up your own mind? And if you do stay in the
Cabinet but continue campaigning against a collective Cabinet
decision, you will be sacked immediately.' I do not know what
the small élite group of Bristol activists advised, but Tony Benn
remained, and relatively quietly.

Unfortunately the markets were less convinced than we were
of the virtue of the Government's monetary policy. When I
returned from France sterling was again wobbly; reserves were
disappearing fast and the pound fell to $1·70 in late September.
The *Sunday Times* carried a headline claiming that it had
information that official Government policy was to force sterling
down to $1.50. There had been a leak from the Treasury direct
to the newspaper as I quickly learned from my own *Sunday
Times* contacts – although the Treasury has understandably
always denied as much in public and in private. Needless to say,
the story did not help the currency. Since the markets now
believed that it was official policy to go down to $1·50, why
should anyone hold sterling at $1·70? There was great pressure
to sell and a limit to how much support could be given to the
currency. It was clear that based on present policies we would
not be able either to finance the external deficit or to meet the
money supply targets for the next year. The Chancellor urgently
requested a meeting with the Economic Strategy Committee of
the Cabinet and said that the Government must quickly go to
the IMF for another loan. The previous application in the

summer had been for merely a small stand-by credit facility, much of which had been spent on defending the currency during the summer. Now it was necessary to arrange serious borrowing from the IMF – a measure to which the Cabinet was already committed in principle. The Chancellor also had plans for import deposits placed on seven-day readiness.

For the next three months the Government was dominated by the Cabinet battles over the IMF crisis. My main impressions from that crisis, as with the public expenditure battles earlier in July, were of the excellent quality of the ministerial debate, the tremendous political skill of Mr Callaghan in mobilising, encouraging and maintaining unity among his Ministers, and the remarkable resilience and stamina of Denis Healey (although he seemed virtually to collapse at one point and the possibility of appointing a new Chancellor was floated). At the end Mr Callaghan emerged very dominant and remained so until the Winter of Discontent in 1979.

The basic economic problem creating the crisis was one of deficits. Domestically, the PSBR was above forecast and money growth was running well above the Treasury's (unpublished) 12 per cent target – monetarism already secretly ruled and we were failing the basic monetarist test. Externally, the trade deficit had widened alarmingly and there was no way we could finance it. The City would not buy gilts, the foreign markets would not hold sterling, and the IMF refused to give any more loans without a further dose of expenditure cuts as evidence of self-discipline. That was the price which had to be paid to obtain each of those essential forms of financial support.

Actually the crisis was in many ways a short-run one. Over the longer term the deflationary policies already introduced – the public expenditure cuts in July and the incomes policy now firmly and successfully in place – would probably have been enough to maintain a reasonable equilibrium. In fact, judged by the newly fashionable monetary criteria the Labour Government's record was relatively good. In terms of money supply growth our percentage increase (10.6 per cent in the past twelve months and 22.1 per cent since taking office in 1974) was better than any other major Western country with the exception of West Germany. Most independent economic forecasters were predicting that the balance of payments was moving slowly towards a surplus. With unemployment continuing to rise, there was actually no economic justification for further deflation – especially as the Treasury's PSBR forecast of £11 billion for 1977–8 was £2 billion higher than the other current forecasts, creating suspicions in our minds that the amount had been inflated to create an atmosphere of crisis enabling the Treasury to 'bounce' large cuts through Ministers. (The Policy Unit submitted to the Prime Minister in November an analysis of the Treasury PSBR forecasts made since we came to office: each seriously underestimated the severity of the developing recession and the growth of unemployment and had a margin of error much greater than the present level of cuts being demanded. We therefore argued that it would be unwise to make immediate major policy changes on the basis of an over-precise interpretation of highly fallible Treasury forecasts.) However, the issue was a question of confidence rather than arguments about monetary forecasts. There was no hope of the current policies being given time to work. The currency was under tremendous pressure and something had to be done; the only remaining question was which measures were necessary.

Interestingly, in view of later developments after the Conservatives returned to power in 1979, the IMF crisis provided a first opportunity for some (although not all) people in the Treasury and in the Bank of England to take the opportunity to try to change the whole economic stance which had characterised all British governments since the Second World War. The first major push took place during the crisis to secure a massive switch of resources from the public to the private sector. The broad policies which are now characterised as 'Thatcherism', together with the now familiar language, were in fact launched in primitive form at Mr Callaghan in 1976 from the Treasury, from the Bank, and above all from the IMF and sections of the US Treasury. Had the Prime Minister accepted the original IMF proposals, there would not have been much more for Mrs Thatcher to do on the public sector front.

By the autumn of 1976 the crisis was not, politically speaking, about the principle of whether to have a further big package of cuts in public expenditure. A majority of the Cabinet were

agreed on that issue; all but the small group of left-wing
Ministers agreed that it had to be done. The Prime Minister's
advisers in No. 10 were also agreed on the basic principle. The
question was about the scale of such cuts. The initial suggestion
which was floated from the IMF and the Treasury in the late
autumn of 1976 was for £5 billion of cuts spread over the next
two years. This was a reduction in both absolute and percentage
terms on a scale which even Mrs Thatcher in her later
knife-wielding heyday never ever achieved and had Mr Callaghan accepted and implemented these huge cuts in full, it
would certainly have caused a major economic recession.
Equally certainly, his Labour Government would have been
destroyed because such a measure would have involved the
reversal of many of the policies which Labour had advocated
and introduced since 1964. The issues at stake were serious
because the last thing the Prime Minister wanted was to alienate
the supporters of his own party and destroy its political *raison
d'être*. Mr Callaghan's very great personal contribution was to
resist the excessive demands being made by the IMF and the
Treasury for a more modest and sensible package of cuts. He
and all those around him accepted that there had to be a package
but he wanted it to be the ultimate package which would prove
sufficient to restore confidence in sterling without being so
recessionary as to destroy his Government.

I should point out that we were not being paranoid in 1976 in
our suspicion that the IMF was capable of launching economic
'remedies' which could destroy governments (especially governments of the left). A year later in November 1977 the IMF
mission to Portugal (including a senior member of the 1976
mission to the UK) refused to grant a credit tranche to the
socialist minority government led by Mr Soares because he
would not make immediate savage economies which would
certainly have brought down his administration and allowed
back into power the old anti-democratic parties of the far right.
Internal IMF briefing, which we saw among diplomatic papers
in Downing Street, at the time stated quite brutally that the IMF
policy was to create a foreign exchange crisis over the next two
months. The IMF staff explicitly asked the Western Governments of the United States, Germany, Japan and Britain to

withhold financial and economic aid in order to create a foreign exchange crisis which would bring the Soares Government to its knees and so force it to accept the harsh IMF prescriptions. No innocent on the international network, Mr Callaghan was absolutely furious on learning this; he instructed the Chancellor to have no part in such a shabby conspiracy and to contact his French, German and American opposite numbers to request them to take a similar view. The Prime Minister viewed the IMF mission to London in 1976 without paranoia but equally without any delusions about its possible motives.

Actually much of October and November were spent in a kind of phoney war. Papers describing the deteriorating economic situation were circulated to Cabinet Ministers. The Chancellor explained these papers and Ministers expressed concern, but no conclusions were reached because everybody was waiting for the next move. The IMF team slipped quietly into a secret London hotel in November, led by a Dutchman called Witteveen, and negotiations with the Cabinet took place via the Treasury. The £5 billion of flesh to be extracted in 1977–9 in return for the IMF loan and seal of approval was revealed to Ministers at the end of November. When the Cabinet sensibly declined to accept the offer the Treasury retreated somewhat bruised and did not actually return with any more proposals for some time. There followed a tense hiatus because although Ministers had sensibly decided not to commit political suicide, the fact remained that without the IMF loan and seal of approval the Government was almost certainly sunk (or would have to retreat into 'fortress Britain').

However, the discussions with the IMF continued at various levels. Most of these were conducted secretly by top Treasury and Bank officials. The Chancellor then reported the broad lines of debate to the Prime Minister, although on at least one occasion the IMF directors came to No. 10 to see the Prime Minister personally to try to break the impasse. This curious shadow-boxing continued for several weeks, during which time Ministers were kept very much in the dark. They had held only their one initial Cabinet discussion and, having rejected the opening proposals, they did not officially know (rumours aside) what was going on between the IMF and the Treasury, or between the Prime Minister, the Chancellor and the IMF. We in the Policy Unit knew everything that was going on because I read the papers and minutes of meetings which were put in the Prime Minister's box and we were therefore able to brief the Prime Minister regularly on developments. It was a very tense time and there can be no doubt that if the IMF had gone away and announced that it was impossible to reach an agreement with us on a loan, the markets would have reacted with panic and sterling would have fallen through the floor. The result of this would have been even bigger public expenditure cuts than those being proposed, or the Government would have had to adopt protection.

The Prime Minister took over the handling of the crisis from the moment the Cabinet rejected the first Treasury paper setting out the initial IMF proposals. Mr Callghan told me that his object was to elicit the lowest cuts package which the IMF could accept whilst maintaining credibility in the money markets. He then pressed the IMF hard, both through the Chancellor and in personal discussion with Witteveen. After his final meeting with the IMF director in early December, the Prime Minister told me that he had successfully persuaded the IMF to ask for smaller cuts but that the minimum had been reached. His political job now was to persuade his Cabinet to agree to an amount close to that minimum. Mr Callaghan said: 'Right, now we have a deal and we must settle.' He privately talked to two of his Cabinet rebels, Crosland and Lever. He had previously been friendly and tolerant towards their resistance to a cuts package, but this time he was brief and very blunt, more or less ordering them to support the improved package which was coming forward. Mr Callaghan asked me to set the Policy Unit to work on producing possible cuts packages which would achieve the required cuts in a form that would be politically acceptable to Ministers and that would have the minimum recessionary impact. The Prime Minister knew from long experience that the political dimension was usually missing from the Treasury's presentation of even commendable policies. Invariably it would come forward with a list of expenditure cuts which no Labour Government could conceivably accept for political reasons, or which totally reversed major manifesto commitments, thus meaning that some Minister would either have to speak out against them or resign. I could never understand this lack of 'political feel' in Treasury papers as not all the Great George Street mandarins were innocents; certainly the Downing Street civil servants, some of whom came on loan from the Treasury, were very perceptive on the political aspects of policy. Perhaps the Treasury decided to leave seamy politics to others and to concentrate on trying to solve the economic questions. Anyway, the Policy Unit produced an alternative package of cuts which met Mr Callaghan's suggested minimum net total of £2 billion – still below the minimum figure indicated by the IMF but the amount which he believed Ministers might find acceptable. The Unit's proposed package was for £3 billion of gross cuts in 1977–9, £1 billion of which would be used for the launch of a major investment programme. In economic terms, this would cut the PSBR to £9 billion. Politically, it would minimise the employment consequences and, on the plus side, would boost investment. The Prime Minister expressed satisfaction at our suggestions and asked the Chancellor to include them in the proposals to be put to Cabinet.

Mr Callaghan called two Cabinet meetings early in December and with the Chancellor he put forward his own final compromise package of £2 billion in cuts – a firm £1 billion of cuts in 1977–8 and an estimated £1 billion in the following year. By putting his own authority fully behind the package, as well as by brutally reminding ministerial colleagues that the alternative would almost certainly mean the end of his Government, he won Cabinet support. At first the IMF was reluctant to accept this small offering, but by taking the initiative in putting a modestly good offer on the table Mr Callaghan had outmanoeuvred the IMF officials: if they refused they would precipitate a crisis. They had no alternative but to accept, and Mr Callaghan had secured the compromise he wanted.

Mr Callaghan's achievement in 1976 was quite remarkable. He had delivered a much smaller IMF cuts package than expected to his Cabinet, and he had delivered his Cabinet's approval to the IMF. By skilful handling he kept the Cabinet united through prolonged and difficult negotiations. He delivered sympathy and support to his Chancellor – something Mr

Callaghan felt that he had rarely received himself as Chancellor in the 1960s when he had to fight for his own support. He took a close interest in the details of the agreement and he received a great deal of briefing – in the Policy Unit we submitted several briefs a week – and was in constant discussions with the Chancellor.

At the end of this long battle in early December Mr Callaghan succumbed to a bad attack of bronchitis. He retired to bed, but continued to involve himself in the detail of the final stages of the agreement. Most important was the Letter of Intent which the recipient nation always gives to the IMF, setting out its commitment to the new economic measures and monetary targets which had been agreed. It seemed to me very important to scrutinise the small print on this document in case some nasty provisions and unnecessarily harsh conditions had been slipped in at the last moment. During the final week I telephoned the Treasury on several occasions asking for a draft of this document, but I was repeatedly told that it was not yet ready. On the Friday I was informed that there was a typing problem; the draft had still not yet officially arrived at Downing Street when I prepared to leave for the weekend towards 8.00 pm. One of the Private Office civil servants (who was immensely helpful to us in the Policy Unit throughout this crisis) came into my office and asked whether I had yet received the draft Letter of Intent. When I explained that I had not, he said that it was probably true the Treasury often did have typing problems, but, although it was not officially his business, he personally felt that it would be helpful to the Prime Minister if I were now to go into the Private Office and look in the special small box which was among the boxes of papers which were being prepared for the Prime Minister's weekend reading. I took his advice, whereupon I found a document with a covering note headed International Monetary Fund Letter of Intent. I made a photocopy and immediately began to study the paper. The terms were extremely tough, much tougher than had been agreed with the Prime Minister as far as detailed monetary targets were concerned. The imposition of tight ceilings on both the PSBR and on Domestic Credit Expansion (the increase in domestic money supply before making allowance for balance of payments effects) seemed to rule out any possibility of reflation before the next election and even made it likely that we would be forced to trigger off a fresh round of deflationary cuts in order to meet these targets: I was very angry and left both the Prime Minister and the Treasury in no doubt as to my views.

That weekend I lived in No. 10 – leaving only to play football for the House of Commons team on the Saturday afternoon – and worked on the Letter of Intent together with Gavyn Davies, the Policy Unit's brilliant economic adviser, whose capacity for work and grasp of complex detail were quite remarkable. Mr Callaghan remained in bed upstairs in the flat recovering from his illness, and was in constant touch with the Chancellor. The Prime Minister was very severe with Mr Healey over the telephone and secured a number of important changes in the Letter of Intent, including the loosening of the ceilings on monetary growth. We also argued against the Treasury's demand that the sale of BP's shares should not, as an asset sale, be used to reduce the PSBR (this is ironic in view of the Treasury's later insistence that Mrs Thatcher's massive privatisation programme should be used to reduce the PSBR). It was immensely satisfying to work with Mr Callaghan as Prime Minister in situations such as this. If he thought his advisers were being too niggling (as we sometimes were), he would say quite bluntly, 'That is enough, Bernard, you are being too suspicious, you just cannot question everything.' If, on the other hand, he was convinced that we had made a valid point he would move into action with very punchy support. He could be extremely tough and I would not have wanted to be on the wrong end of one of his telephone calls. However, it certainly meant that, once committed, he made sure that things happened.

The IMF agreement formally entrenched monetarism in Labour's economic policy-making, although it really only made public what was already happening privately in Whitehall. The monetary targets, previously kept private in the Treasury, were now to be published. Interestingly, the machinery of government soon began to adjust to accommodate this change in economic ideas and priorities. The existing Whitehall procedures for discussing economic policy were Keynesian in nature, in the sense that there were Cabinet Committees to discuss conventional macro-economic policy, and also to discuss micro-policies relating to industry, but nowhere were the monetary factors – such as interest rates, exchange rates and the money supply figures – considered by Ministers. Even within the Treasury the main emphasis was towards the basic fiscal stance and whether demand needed to be engineered up or down; the monetary division was much smaller and until the mid-1970s seemed to be primarily a post-box for communications with the Bank of England, which was considered to understand and to be in charge of monetary matters.

However, as the monetarist approach moved to the centre stage of government thinking, so the machinery of government was forced to respond. The Treasury raised the seniority of its own officials on the monetary side (incidentally setting up tensions with the Bank over where the primacy lay). But the key question was how to involve Ministers. Because the Government's economic success or failure might be determined by what its monetary policies were, it seemed to us necessary to involve Ministers in determining their own fate. The No. 10 advisers, initiated by the very able Principal Private Secretary, Kenneth Stowe, discussed which new procedures would be appropriate. A conventional Cabinet Committee was ruled out, as questions of proposed actions on interest rates or on sterling exchange rates were too sensitive to be discussed in a wide committee with circulation of papers. Instead, a secret committee called 'The Seminar' was formed, in which normal rights of ministerial attendance did not apply. It was a small 'mixed' committee, containing ministers and officials, under the chairmanship of the Prime Minister. Others who regularly attended were the Chancellor, the Permanent Secretary and the External Finance Second Secretary from the Treasury, the Governor of the Bank of England, Harold Lever (then Chancellor of the Duchy of Lancaster), the Secretary to the Cabinet, the Principal Private Secretary and myself. Occasionally the President of the Board of Trade or other officials would attend if their presence was relevant to the agenda. It was interesting that the Bank of England regularly attended a meeting of Cabinet Ministers – rather in the way that the Chiefs of Staff attended the Cabinet Defence Committee.

This 'Seminar' committee met regularly in 1977–9 in order to discuss the major decisions on interest rates and sterling. During this time the Prime Minister was particularly concerned to prevent sterling from rising and so creating unemployment, but all attempts to 'cap' sterling failed because the Government's overall economic and monetary policy was so successful during 1977 and 1978 (it was not even necessary fully to implement the second year's IMF cuts). The general confidence about the economy fed through to sterling and foreigners became once again willing to buy. It was also clear that the Bank of England was very happy to have a strong currency operating against inflation. The Prime Minister often put pressure on the Governor, Gordon Richardson, but refused to allow the committee to issue him with instructions. These two men always treated one another with considerable respect; after one particularly sharp discussion, when the Governor was being at his most impressively and courteously obstinate, Mr Callaghan said to me: 'He has to do his job. I either back him or sack him, and I am certainly not going to sack him.' Although it is presumably conducted in a different style, the 'Seminar' machinery for considering monetary questions was continued by Mrs Thatcher after 1979, when monetarism reached its brief period of excessive influence. For Mr Callaghan it became one more area of central government in which during 1977–8 he exercised his dominance over the conduct of policy. The IMF crisis had given him the opportunity he needed to establish that dominance.

5

Housing, Education, Health and the Professions

Economic problems dominated the time of Downing Street in the 1970s because without economic success we were bound to fail elsewhere. However, the Labour Government had many other concerns, especially in the fields of social policy, which were closer than economic concerns to the hearts of Labour supporters. More people vote for the Labour party because they want better homes, schools and hospitals than because they wish to see versions of Keynesian or Marxist economics implemented. It is therefore appropriate to review what was attempted and achieved in these and other non-economic policy areas.

Housing was traditionally a policy area from which the Labour party drew political strength. Its national commitment to devote massive resources to public housing, together with the activity of Labour local authorities in rehousing a significant proportion of the population, had created a mini-electorate of council house tenants who had provided the core of Labour's support since Herbert Morrison's great successes with the London County Council before the Second World War. Apart from a brief period in the 1950s when Harold Macmillan, as Conservative Minister of Housing, carried out an essentially Labour policy of massively extending public housing, the Conservatives have often been on the defensive in the housing debate. However, by the early 1970s this situation was clearly changing. In the two elections of 1974 (and much more dramatically in 1979) it was clear that Labour was losing its solid support on the council housing estates. From early in the 1974

Government we in Downing Street tried to grapple with this political threat, without success. It was one of several issues where the Labour party was becoming totally out of touch with the wishes of ordinary people in the street, including the vast majority of its own supporters. Labour's housing policy was dominated by dogma and the vested interests of a minority of activists whose power was based on the local authority building departments and who were out of touch with and apparently completely unconcerned with the wishes of British families. It was one more of many examples where it was to be shown that in a majority democracy such as ours it is politically fatal for a government to follow the policies of a minority élite of party activists.

The Secretaries of State responsible for housing were first Anthony Crosland (1974–6) and then Peter Shore (1976–9). The range of responsibilities they held under the title of Minister for the Environment were broad-based in that they covered the extensive minefields of local government, but their political success or failure was usually judged in the party by what took place on the housing front. The problems which faced them in that area were enormous. Although, following improvements to the size and condition of Britain's housing stock, there was no clear-cut national housing shortage, there remained serious shortfalls in housing both in particular areas and for particular groups. Inner cities were then, as now, the areas worst affected. Even when housing of an 'average' type was plentiful, the young, the old, the single, the single-parent family, the disabled and the unskilled with large families often experienced difficulty in finding accommodation which was suitable and affordable. (The contraction of the private rented sector, aggravated by Labour's own legislation controlling rents and tenure, made the situation worse.) In dealing with these shortages, the Government was constrained by financial considerations. Instead of spending more on new buildings – and especially on the most fruitful area of refurbishing older properties – the Government was forced to cut back on expenditure for all the reasons of economic imperative set out in the previous two chapters. Actually the question of housing finance was particularly complex. Subsidies and rebates were given to different groups of council tenants in various, often illogical, ways. By 1976 revenues from council house rents recovered only 43 per cent of housing costs, compared with nearly 80 per cent in 1970. Above all, local authority building was excessively expensive due to the almost incredible inefficiency of most local government building departments.

Anthony Crosland in 1974 quickly set up a Housing Finance Review, the purpose of which was to carry out a radical and far-reaching survey of the chaotic state of housing finance and to produce some action and policies before the next election. However, within the Department of the Environment itself there were bitter clashes between regular officials, outside advisers and economists and other Whitehall departments refused to co-operate. Furthermore, there were accusations that the Secretary of State was himself not giving a strong enough lead. Originally promised for the autumn of 1975, a year later the Review had run into the sand and ended as a feeble package. The Department of the Environment showed equal timidity in the wider field of local authority finance which had also been the subject of the recent excellent Layfield Report. Officials were resistant to the intensive efforts made by Harold Lever and myself, with strong backing from the Prime Minister in the summer of 1974, to establish a National Housing Finance Corporation and to use public subsidy to prevent sudden rises in mortgage rates during a temporary period of building society illiquidity.

Actually a number of commendable initiatives were eventually launched by Peter Shore towards the end of the Government's tenure. He mastered the appalling complexities of the inner city problem and made as much progress to redistribute resources towards these run-down areas as was possible within the constraints of public expenditure. (The renovation of Glasgow's East End was an example in Scotland of what was intended for many British cities.) He also pursued the idea of a Tenant's Charter, which was excellent in itself and was also a desirable if rare move in the direction of caring for the long-suffering tenant consumers of public housing, as well as the privileged and inefficient producers and managers of housing on the local authority pay rolls.

However, no progress at all was made on one central political issue about which I personally felt very strongly, namely that of offering council tenants the right to buy their own homes. The evidence of public feeling on this matter was overwhelming. Tenants made it clear to canvassers on the doorsteps at elections and every opinion poll and social survey revealed its growing importance. At the 1974 elections any Labour politician with ears to listen could not but be aware of the strength of feeling existing on council estates. A National Economic Development Office (NEDO) survey in January 1976 found that people gave the extension of home ownership priority over all other proposed strategic aims of housing policy (including increasing the supply). Among council tenants 64 per cent mentioned this as being a very high priority and one-third wanted to own their own council home. By 1978 the opinion polls showed Labour trailing 8 per cent behind the Conservatives on housing policy and 15 per cent of Labour voters preferred Conservative policies because of the question of home ownership. In the 1979 election the Conservative promise to allow and encourage council tenants to acquire their own homes was a major factor in the defection of Labour voters, especially in the new towns and the city estates. Not every tenant wanted to buy his or her own particular house; but they wanted the freedom of choice to exist, especially for their children.

Shortly after entering Downing Street in 1974, the Press Secretary, Joe Haines (who had long experience on the housing committee of a local authority) and I discussed how to reverse the political tide on housing policy and we held several meetings of the Policy Unit to review the whole field. The most fruitful specific suggestions were made by Joe, with major contributions by the enormously able No. 10 Private Secretary, Robin Butler, who sat in on all of these meetings. Our conclusions* were to recommmend a major extension of home ownership into the council sector and we made proposals for a series of alternative schemes of 'life leases' under which existing tenants would be offered the right to buy their council homes after a certain qualifying period of residence. The price of such a purchase

---

* Described in Joe Haines's book *The Politics of Power.*

would be calculated as a modest multiple of current rent and might be reduced after long residence. We judged that the schemes would not have reduced the amount of immediately available council stock because most purchasers would have occupied their existing homes as tenants anyway. Moreover, the public housing stock would not be reduced over the longer term because one of our schemes proposed that on the departure or death of the purchasers (and perhaps one generation of his or her descendants) the house would be re-purchased by the council for re-letting and eventual re-sale. Thus the council tenant would acquire the right to own a house for life and enjoy the capital appreciation while the council would receive an immediate capital payment to invest in new accommodation and would no longer have to carry the enormous burden of repairs and maintenance on the accommodation once it was owner-occupied; that is, until it exercised its option to reacquire the property when the life leaseholder died or wished to sell. The proposed schemes were to be offered permissively to local authorities, who would be free to choose not to introduce the new measures if their local housing situation would in any way be harmed by them. Basically the idea was to widen tenants' choice without eroding the local housing stock.

The package of four schemes for 'life leaseholders' was put to Prime Minister Wilson in October 1975 and he welcomed the suggestions enthusiastically. Mr Wilson wrote to me: 'Yes, this is a fascinating study. The question now is how to proceed,' and, suggesting that the Policy Unit paper be sent to Chancellor Healey, the Secretary of State for the Environment (Tony Crosland) and to Harold Lever 'for immediate reactions', he concluded: 'What we do not want is for it to get lost in the official machine for months.' Following this ministerial discussion we reformulated our proposals bearing in mind our colleagues' criticisms and suggestions and resubmitted them in December. We then had a series of detailed discussions with officials in the Department of the Environment, who were very positive and helpful. At this stage one of the schemes was significantly changed and our agreed paper was submitted to a Cabinet Committee (MISC 127) chaired by the Prime Minister in March 1976. Ministers there concluded that the political and financial advantages were sufficient to justify asking officials to make further progress on detailed drafting of specific policies. However, this progress did not materialise, partly because the resignation of Mr Wilson, who had been an enthusiastic supporter, inevitably led to delay but also because opposition was mobilised in the higher echelons of the Department of the Environment, where some Ministers and their advisers were antagonistic, or lacked the courage to take on the political opposition within the Labour party. Anthony Crosland and his advisers (although not most of his regular officials) were particularly disappointing in their reactions. The left wing of the Labour party began to mobilise hostility to what they saw as a threat to their local authority power bases. Although they themselves personally often enjoyed the pleasures and benefits of living in their own private Hampstead homes, they were dogmatically committed to denying those pleasures and benefits to council tenants. I had endless arguments about housing policy with party colleagues, and in particular with special advisers at the Departments of Environment and Energy, but these talks always ended with them saying that they could not support a policy which diminished the public housing stock – despite my repeated explanations that our policy was permissive and was specifically designed not to do that. Ironically, the final outcome of their dogmatically resisting the public will and thus conceding the initiative in this area to Mrs Thatcher, was that they ensured the triumph of the Conservatives who subsequently were able to introduce policies which did sadly and seriously diminish the public housing stock.

Thus our Policy Unit housing initiative was defeated. When Peter Shore finally drafted an official statement on the Government's position on the sale of council houses in late 1978 it was phrased in a way which would delight a few thousand activists on the Labour left and alienate the hundreds of thousands of council tenant voters who wanted more freedom. The Government's affirmation of qualified support for home ownership clearly applied only to the private sector. I saw an early draft of this statement and briefed the Prime Minister on the danger of newspaper headlines stating 'Labour says No to selling council homes to tenants'. Thus the way was prepared for Mrs Thatcher's success in the 1979 election with the hundreds of thousands of young voters whose ambition was to own their own homes. Undoubtedly, had there been more resources to spend on housing, our policies would have enjoyed a greater degree of success and popularity. However, the heart of the problem was that the Government was trapped in the out-dated prejudices of its own party organisation and because of this we failed to appreciate the changing spirit and priorities of our own natural supporters.

Another area of increasing concern during the 1970s was education. Both major parties – Labour inclining towards ever-increasing expenditure and a liberal permissiveness in the classrooms, and the Conservatives opting out of the state system and strengthening the élite sector – were out of touch with broad public opinion as frequently tested in surveys. The majority of the public were actually content with the basic *structure* of education as had been established through the introduction of the comprehensive system. However, they wanted to see a more disciplined approach to reinforcing traditional standards in the hope of producing a literate, numerate and employable young generation.

In actual fact, education was surprisingly rarely at the centre of the Labour Cabinet's attention; no educational matter was on the agenda of Harold Wilson's Cabinet throughout our first year in government and in the following years it was still a rare occurrence. (The regular Downing Street civil servants told me that this was true of other governments as well. Certainly the post of Secretary of State for Education is normally a junior one and Sir Keith Joseph's controversial tenure was a rare example of a senior occupant, presumably reflecting Mrs Thatcher's desire to introduce radical changes which would have been beyond the political power of a more junior figure.) Between 1974–9 the Labour Ministers of Education were Reg Prentice (who seemed inactive), Fred Mulley (who was much more able than many realised but was not a leading member of the Cabinet) and Shirley Williams (a rising but still junior politician). The problem for all of them was that their department had little power. Education policy was conducted by the local authorities and the teachers' unions with the Department of

Education, as Harold Wilson once commented to me, being little more than a post-box between the two. A further problem was that each Minister was burdened with party policy commitments which were based on the assumption that all education problems would be solved by simply throwing money at them or, to be more precise, giving the cash to the teachers' unions. In fact the latter, and especially the National Union of Teachers, had become a major part of the problem. In all my many dealings with the NUT at that time I never once heard mention of education or children. The union's prime objective appeared to be to secure ever decreasing responsibilities and hours of work for its members and it seemed that the ideal NUT world would be one where teachers and children never entered a school at all – and the executive of the NUT would be in a permanent conference session at a comfortable seaside hotel. This fact was very sad to me personally, as when young I had owed everything to the total dedication of a succession of marvellous teachers in the state school system.

The first serious education question to concern Downing Street (it did not go to Cabinet) was the proposal in January 1975 to set up a committee of enquiry into the management of schools (later established as the Taylor Committee). The initial terms of reference referred to the interests of the local community, itself a welcome new departure, but characteristically made no mention of parents (or for that matter of children). I briefed the Prime Minister in support of setting up the committee of enquiry but added a request that parents be considered specifically as a separate legitimate body to be consulted. Although the Department of Education replied that this would deeply offend the teachers' unions, my proposal was adopted.

This was a minor skirmish. There was another in 1975 when Downing Street intervened, with the full support of the Cabinet Secretary, to secure a change at the top of the Department of Education. The existing Permanent Secretary was transferred to a more appropriate department and was replaced by James Hamilton, who had a background in science and engineering and whom I had previously found encouragingly positive on Cabinet Office Committees. However, we had to wait for a new Prime Minister in order to establish education properly on the agenda. The opportunity came with the arrival of James Callaghan as Prime Minister in April 1976. The only Premier born in the twentieth century who had not benefited from attending university, he revealed a deep concern for the quality of education available to Britain's youth. He was also never afraid to take on the Whitehall establishment.

During his first Easter holiday at Chequers I sent him a long paper on the possible style and policy interests which he might adopt as Prime Minister. I suggested that although it was undesirable for a Prime Minister to meddle in every department's affairs, it would be no bad thing if he were to identify a few areas of policy of genuine interest to himself where he could try to make an impact, and I put forward education as a leading candidate.

Mr Callaghan responded quickly and positively by asking the Policy Unit to draft a major speech for him to deliver at an early opportunity – which, in the event, came about when he visited Ruskin College, Oxford. I worked on this speech with Elizabeth Arnott, the bright education specialist in the Policy Unit, and in it I included all the feelings which I shared with the Prime Minister on the need for more rigorous educational standards, for greater monitoring and accountability of teachers, for greater concentration on the basic skills of literacy and numeracy, and for giving greater priority to technical, vocational and practical education (between 1967–73 the number of engineering students in Britain had increased by only 5 per cent while sociology increased by 38 per cent, theology by 51 per cent and general arts courses by 169 per cent). We also supported the allocation of more resources to mature students and stepping up the use of educational plant. Mr Callaghan made many personal positive amendments to the draft, the basic principle of which was improving the quality as opposed to the quantity of education at a time when resources were constrained.

The Ruskin speech, in which Mr Callaghan called for a Great Debate to begin on education, was delivered to a small and informal audience in north Oxford in October 1976. It received massive and generally friendly coverage as it struck a chord with public opinion. Mr Callaghan's sentiments clearly echoed the deep concerns of many parents (although they offended many people in the party, a surprising number of whom were actually childless, while those who had children frequently resorted to private education). The education profession reacted, predictably, with less generosity than the public. The NUT was furious. The Department of Education was shocked. Shirley Williams, who had just taken over as Secretary of State from Fred Mulley, was unhappy that the Prime Minister had trespassed into her ministerial territory, opened a can of worms, and then left her to deal with the consequences. The Senior Chief Inspector of Schools asked to see me and she conducted a thorough investigation of my motives and objectives (although I sensed that she and the Inspectorate were secretly happy that somebody in power had at last talked about the real educational problems which they saw every day at classroom level).

When the Prime Minister, who had held a long discussion with Fred Mulley about education problems earlier in the summer of 1976, asked the Department of Education and Science (DES) to produce a 'green' discussion paper following up the themes which he had identified in his Ruskin speech, officials made it clear that they were not enthusiastic. They moved slowly and when the draft green paper arrived in June 1977 it was sparse in content and deeply complacent in tone. Only three of its 200 paragraphs were devoted to the criticisms and problems facing our schools; on a quick reading it was therefore possible to conclude that nothing was wrong with British education. There were only three bland paragraphs on standards and on discipline; and such important questions as the content of the curriculum and the role of the school in the community were virtually ducked altogether. Parents were discussed only in terms of their being on the receiving end of information, rather than as participants with a personal interest in the education system. Finally, the draft green paper made only one hidden reference to the Ruskin speech and appeared to ignore the debate which had followed. The paper represented Whitehall at its self-satisfied, condescending and unimaginative worst. However, at the same time I was contacted by some of the younger officials at the DES who said that they shared our view of their department's attitude; they too wanted a more positive approach and they hoped that we in Downing Street would insist on improvements. Shirley Williams also indicated that she was willing to take a more radical line provided that she could rely on continuing political support from the Prime Minister when the unions inevitably kicked up rough. We were encouraged by these responses and briefed the Prime Minister to insist on a more positive and radical approach. This message was accepted internally if not always publicly (little change was made to the green paper in its final form), and the department slowly moved its stance to one more in line with the principles and proposals laid out in Mr Callaghan's Ruskin speech.

The Prime Minister had certainly made his mark on a chosen policy area, as envisaged when he came into office. Ironically, the Ruskin speech became the Whitehall blueprint for what Sir Keith Joseph later attempted, and partly achieved, under Mrs Thatcher's subsequent administration, although from quite different motives. Our intention had been to make the educational system meet the needs of education and serve the children of this country, rather than to effect cutbacks in public expenditure. Had Labour enjoyed the time and demonstrated the will necessary to implement the Ruskin proposals, I believe they would have made teaching and schooling (the most important of human endeavours) a more satisfactory experience, without the battles and demoralisation which resulted from the later tactics of confrontation in the field of education. However, one cannot be sure of this because in Britain the resistance of professional vested interests to radical change of any kind is so great and so instinctive. It may be that we need regular changes of government so that each ruling party can in turn attack the entrenched conservatism of the other party's supporting vested interests.

Mr Callaghan also showed considerable personal concern in the area of the National Health Service. His wife, Audrey, was very active as a Governor of Great Ormond Street Hospital and his youngest daughter was a doctor's wife; consequently there was plenty of feedback within his family. A few months after becoming Prime Minister he summoned his Secretary of State for Health and Social Services, David Ennals, to his study in Downing Street and conducted a very thorough scrutiny of the department's affairs.

The problems of the NHS ranged from the acute to the merely chronic. Since the Conservative reorganisation in the early 1970s, which led to a virtual doubling of the numbers of administrative and clerical staff between 1970 and 1976, the NHS had become smothered with bureaucracy. The doctors were unhappy, resenting this growing bureaucracy and also feeling that their clinical freedom was being restricted by interference from the DHSS to save money by limiting tests and prescriptions. Many older and smaller hospitals were being closed, which upset local communities. The numbers on the waiting lists for hospital treatment had grown to 500,000 by 1976. The policy of community care for the mentally handicapped required more resources than were available, as did the emphasis given by the young Minister of Health, David Owen, to preventive medicine. Indeed, the genuine demand for extra facilities in the NHS at a time when the Government was being forced to cut public expenditure was the biggest overall problem, for which there was no immediate practical solution.

Although David Ennals was not a powerful Minister in the way that his predecessor, Barbara Castle, had been, he was a caring man and, because he had been a long-time supporter of Mr Callaghan, he had some access to the Prime Minister. David Ennals's able junior Ministers, Jack Ashley and Alf Morris, were totally devoted to the welfare of the poor, the sick and the disabled. Indeed, they were two of the most genuinely decent politicians I have ever met. (Perhaps the greatest satisfaction I enjoyed in Downing Street was in helping to provide Palantype equipment in the chamber of the Commons to enable Jack, who is totally deaf, to follow the proceedings.) No. 10 also helped to get resources to found a new institute for research on deafness, to which Jack was very committed. David Owen also brought professional knowledge and great administrative drive to his post as Minister of State for Health until moving to the Foreign Office in January 1977; and all of these Ministers were supported by a superb Permanent Secretary in Patrick Nairne.

Mr Callaghan personally intervened in the discussions of public expenditure for 1976–7, securing an offer of an extra £50 million for the NHS which produced a most curious response from the DHSS. Making the offer in our letter from No. 10, we had stated that the intention was that the extra money would be used to improve patients' care, which was not in itself a surprising objective. However, in his response the Minister said that he was troubled by this condition being imposed, as it might upset the health service trade unions who apparently felt that any extra money should be for their members rather than for patients. (Here was a demonstration of the relevance of the famous episode in the television series 'Yes, Minister' about the award-winning hospital with thousands of staff but no patients.) On this occasion the Prime Minister was forced to hold a meeting in Downing Street with the leaders of the NHS trade unions to explain why his preference was for giving money to treat the sick.

Undaunted, in the following year Mr Callaghan again sought ways to justify providing extra funds to the health service and he asked David Ennals to produce a paper on the NHS crisis with the intention of using it to squeeze more money out of the Treasury. When the paper arrived early in 1978, the Prime Minister asked Sir Kenneth Berrill, the head of the Central Policy Review Staff, and me to do an assessment for him. We found the paper unsatisfactory and generally vague in many ways, but the case for extra resources could not be denied and in this way a little more progress was made.

In some areas, however, we did not even achieve this modest success. When Mr Justice Finer's brilliant report on the problems of single-parent families appeared in 1975, I was unable to persuade Barbara Castle, whose priorities lay elsewhere, to take any interest in implementing its recommendations. It also proved difficult trying to deal with true poverty in British society. The Labour party and the trade unions assumed that poverty coincided with low pay and therefore the best approach was to help the low paid. However, need rather than pay levels was the best criterion. Obviously the low paid were not well off and deserved as much help as possible, but often they were single, young or part-time workers, with responsibility only for themselves. In actual fact, the most poverty lay within large families, in which the single wage earner might not be the lowest paid on the national scale but nevertheless earned insufficient for the care of his family (in many cases the breadwinner would have been better off not working but on national assistance). For this reason our new and improved child allowance scheme introduced in 1978 was vital in mitigating family poverty, although sadly it received little support from some Ministers and from the TUC, who opposed what they called 'a transfer from the wallet to the purse'. To her credit, Mrs Castle, who had excellent special advisers as well as junior Ministers, was a tough protagonist of this scheme and had battered down much of this prejudice by the time she left office in 1976.

When issues fell between or across departmental responsibilities, no single Minister was likely to take them up and the opportunity then arose for Downing Street to take the initiative. The problem of families being hurt by the economic squeeze was one of several such themes pursued by the Policy Unit. In the spring of 1977 Gavyn Davies sent me a devastating minute setting out statistically the disproportionate burdens being carried by families. This arose particularly because a family needed nearly 50 per cent more gross income in order to have the same standard of living as a married couple without children and yet the real value of child support had actually been allowed to fall 10 per cent since 1974. Public sector price rises, particularly school meal charges and bus fares, had also hit families badly.

Identifying increased child support as the most effective means of help, I briefed Mr Callaghan on the problem, suggesting that a special Cabinet Committee be set up to consider how to give help to families. My proposals were very warmly supported by the Cabinet Secretary, John Hunt, and the CPRS co-operated to produce a good consultative document on the problems of the family. The Prime Minister launched the Committee and took a very active part, using the 'family' theme in his speeches and sending a strong personal minute to the Secretary of State for Social Services in which he pressed for the DHSS to give a new stimulus to support for the family. Unfortunately, the initiative eventually ran into the sand because of departmental squabbling and the fact that the Cabinet Committee never clarified its objectives. However, although there were repeated delays in introducing the new child benefit scheme to replace the old, regressive child tax allowances, at least it was put into place before we left office, even though it was introduced at too low a level to meet family needs.

A number of other important social policy themes were pursued using the vehicle of enquiry through royal commissions. One personal worry of mine had long been the amateur approach and conservative influence of the traditional professions in England. The law was an obvious starting place for anyone concerned with blatant, middle-class trade union, monopoly restrictive practices, conducted at the expense of the ordinary citizen. Jack Ashley, a highly professional campaigner on behalf of various breeds of underdog, put down a Commons motion calling for an enquiry into the professions; he secured over a hundred signatures. I then persuaded Mr Wilson (who at the time coined the phrase 'a cheat of lawyers' as a collective description) to set up in 1976 a Royal Commission on Legal Services. (It was originally to be on 'legal practices' but that was felt to be too revealing and provocative.) For my guidance of a very willing Prime Minister I was regularly briefed by two life-long legal friends – Michael Zander, Professor of Law at the London School of Economics, and Anthony Lester QC, then special adviser to the Home Secretary, Roy Jenkins.

The Commission was intended to conduct a radical review into the organisation, training practices and financing of the legal profession – and perhaps for this reason was opposed tooth and nail by the Lord Chancellor's department, acting in its customary role as shop steward for the legal establishment. Mr Wilson overcame this opposition with great firmness and humour and we ensured that some reformists were members of the Commission. However, Mr Wilson resigned shortly afterwards and during the interregnum the Lord Chancellor's department launched in a paper, which was never shown to me, a shrewd counterattack by nominating a very conservative accountant as Chairman. (I had proposed several more radical candidates as Chairman, including Adrian Cadbury, John Freeman, Peter Parker, Asa Briggs and Alec Cairncross, none of whom was part of the vested interest establishment of the professions.) In the event the Commission's report was disappointing and led to little change; the problems which led to its inception are still with us and the two sides of the law industry will some day have to come to grips with them.

The Government's attempts to make a wide-ranging review of the professions gathered pace under Mr Callaghan, focusing in quick succession on the City, the medical practitioners and on engineering. The enquiry into the working of our financial institutions was placed in the hands of ex-Premier Harold Wilson, who had always seemed intrigued by but innocent of the operations within the City. (He asked for me to leave No. 10 to act as Secretary to his Commission but fortunately Mr Callaghan declined.) The Merrison Enquiry into the medical profession reflected the widespread feeling that the NHS was in crisis: it offered the hope of distinguishing the greater from the lesser needs among the clamour of claims for more expenditure on health.

The idea of an enquiry into engineering had been in the air for some time. It was supported by the Institute of Electrical Engineers, the President of the Institute of Mechanical Engineers, the TUC and John Lyons, the able General Secretary of the Power Engineers' Union, with whom I was in regular contact on a basis of friendship. The case for an enquiry was strong. The collapse of the British engineering industry into uncompetitiveness and bankruptcy was argument enough, quite apart from the inadequacies of training, social status and rewards for engineers in Britain which were notorious. An area of particular concern to me personally was production engineering which, at the sharp end of the profession, received the least resources and status, a lamentable characteristic of British industry. Since 1970 no more than 275 production engineers per year were awarded degrees by the British higher education system, and that number was declining (moreover nearly half of these were overseas students who would return to their home countries). Given the Government's and Mr Callaghan's personal commitment to achieve 'industrial regeneration' in Britain, the dire situation in engineering was clearly very relevant and needed attention.

However, for the most part the engineering establishment was strongly opposed to an enquiry into its failures. Fearful of change, the traditional Chartered Institutes mobilised ready support from top officials at the Department of Industry, who had presided disdainfully over the decline of the British engineering industry while protected by their own job security and inflation-proofed pensions from suffering any of the material consequences. Even Prince Philip was wheeled out to speak against an enquiry. At this point, after a conversation with John Lyons, I briefed the Prime Minister on the need to support the side of change. Mr Callaghan was anyway already well apprised of the situation and commented that whenever the old professional establishment united it was always against the wider public interest. In the summer of 1977 he wrote a minute to the Department of Industry stating that the enquiry should be set up; however, the department's response was to explain why it would not be doing so. When I spoke to Eric Varley, the Secretary of State, who had signed the departmental letter, he said he had not read it but had been under the impression that the letter's contents were agreeing to establish the Commission as that was the preference which he had conveyed to officials. He seemed embarrassed that his advisers had contradicted both his and the Prime Minister's wishes and he promised to reverse the situation. As a result, the Commission was set up under the Chairmanship of Sir Monty Finniston, although the subsequent report was not considered until after Labour left office. The Department of Industry then recommended to their new Secretary of State, Sir Keith Joseph, that little action need be taken on most of the Report's main findings with which conclusions he was apparently in agreement. Even had Labour remained in power the probable outcome would not have been very different. It is extremely difficult to introduce change in a society in which most power and vested interest lie with the status quo.

We had a similar disappointment with the Annan Commission Report on broadcasting which recommended the establishment of a new Open Broadcasting Authority for the imminent fourth television channel designed to be less subject to commercial pressures than the existing channel three and with more independent productions than is possible on the BBC. We in Downing Street supported this proposal (although not everything else in the Report) because it promised to bring about a desirable increase in the diversity and accountability of broadcasting in Britain. We also backed the suggestion of a Public Enquiry Board which would embrace a complaints machinery to respond to public criticism (against, for instance, violence and sexual perversion in programmes). These and other recommendations made in the Annan Report were submitted to a Cabinet Committee (GEN 114) at the beginning of 1978. Mr Callaghan took a personal interest in the issue and asked his personal staff to follow events closely – and with good cause. From the beginning the Home Office showed itself (as is often the case with Whitehall departments) to be much closer to the interests of its broadcasting clients than to those of central government. Its initial papers to the Committee, even before ministerial discussion, rejected the main Annan proposals and stated that (1) the new fourth channel should go to the existing IBA and (2) complaints could be left to be handled by the BBC and the ITV authorities themselves. The Ministers, firmly led by the Prime Minister, argued otherwise and also suggested that the BBC should be divided into separate corporations for television and radio. (This was not in the Annan Report but was strongly pressed for by William Rodgers.) Although the Cabinet Committee minutes reflected ministerial wishes, this was far from the case with the subsequent Home Office papers which were written as if no alternative views had been presented. It also emerged at a private meeting I had with a friend who was a senior comptroller at the BBC that the relevant official (and 'secret') Cabinet papers were being shown to the authorities at the BBC and at ITV. My friend described the contents of the official papers and was able to name the Ministers who had dissented from the Home Office proposals; he also commented that although the BBC now recognised that there might have to be a few changes in the policy position which had been previously agreed with the Home Office before Ministers had met, any major changes by Ministers 'would not be acceptable'. In view of the periodic indignation expressed and legal proceedings launched from Whitehall (especially from the Home Office) when secret documents are 'leaked' to the media, it is clear that double standards operate in the application of the Official Secrets Act. As for the Annan Report, ministerial discussions dragged on into the summer, although eventually some compromises were extracted from the Home Office after the Prime Minister despatched Tom McNally (his excellent Political Secretary) and me to the Home Office to hold discussions with the relevant officials. However, we again achieved very little; it was clear that the Home Office was intent on the fourth channel being in some form or other commercial and that the BBC should be protected from radical organisational change. As usual, Whitehall won in the end, although it must be admitted that Channel 4 as it finally emerged has been a success, achieving by a different structure the advocated virtues of independence and diversity which we in No. 10 sought, as well as the commercial financing which the Home Office always advocated.

A great deal of committee time was also devoted to four earlier Commission reports on related areas of publication and the law: the Franks Report on Official Secrets, the Younger Report on Privacy, the Phillimore Report on Contempt and the Faulks Report on Defamation. Some progress was made on these while Roy Jenkins was at the Home Office because he worked hard to get some liberal concessions out of officials and fellow Ministers. The Policy Unit endeavoured to support him, but both Mr Wilson and Mr Callaghan tended to conservatism in these areas. Actually Harold Wilson did try to strike a deal with the press, whereby the media would be granted some relaxation in access to public institutions and official documents in return for a guarantee of greater responsibility and respect for privacy. However, the newspapers would never have been able to deliver and in any case the worst offenders, such as the *Daily Mail* and the Murdoch press, depended on low standards for their commercial success. With the Younger Report, as the general right of privacy was a matter of civil law we had to deal with the Lord Chancellor's Office, as we also did with the Faulks Report. This meant that in both cases the prospects of reform were very poor; the Reports merely gathered dust there. For the Phillimore Report on Contempt it was necessary to liaise with the Scottish Office and the Director of Prosecutions as well as the Lord Chancellor's Office; all three parties were against relaxing the existing law and for delaying consideration of the Commission's recommendations. Although, I tried to persuade Mr Wilson to support Roy Jenkins and push the Lord Chancellor into more positive action in December 1975, I did not get very far.

The Franks Report on reforming the Official Secrets Act was discussed more frequently because of Labour party pressure. It came before a Cabinet Committee (MISC 89) in October 1975 and was then divided in two: the criminal aspects were placed under the auspices of the Home Office and the question of liberalising the publication of official documents was put under the cloak of the Civil Service department. By the time they reported back to Cabinet Committee Mr Callaghan was Prime Minister and, although he was not very sympathetic to change, he gave the issue a fair run in Committee. Although Douglas Allen at the Civil Service department made some characteristically sensible suggestions for increasing public access to non-sensitive documents, the official recommendations on the Official Secrets Act were predictably anti-liberal and came up with even more draconian penalties for wider definitions of breaches of official secrecy. However, the most disappointing feature was to see how many Ministers took a reactionary position on this issue. After Roy Jenkins had resigned in 1976 there was no senior Minister who took a radical stand. The Chancellor and the Treasury were perhaps the most liberal, professing themselves to be perfectly relaxed about the publication of various categories of economic documents which the official papers to the Committee had described as being inviolably secret. However, even after interminable discussions we achieved nothing in this area. It was clear that most people in central government saw only potential embarrassment in revealing to the electorate more about their activities on behalf of the general public. Nobody appeared to believe in the citizen's 'right to know' (including Peter Shore, who had earlier written a book with that title.) Although I had never been a raging radical on this issue, the importance of which is exaggerated by some commentators, I was shocked by the élitism and the unthinking reactionary assumptions behind many of the assertions made against change. A democracy is healthier when citizens are provided with the maximum information on how they are governed. This does not mean publishing everything, but certainly 70 per cent of the documents which passed across my and the Prime Minister's desks could have been published without any ill consequences except boredom to the reader.

A final Commission of Enquiry was the 1976 Radcliffe Report on ministerial memoirs which was a response to the situation following the 1974 judicial decision to allow the publication of the Crossman Diaries. It effectively accepted what were previously considered to be breaches of the Official Secrets Act and attempted to set out the conventions and to regulate the conditions under which Ministers (and presumably their personal advisers) might and might not publish their memoirs. The Report set out a rough 'fifteen-year rule' for memoirs within the thirty-year rule for official documents. However, the handling of the Report within central government was very unsatisfactory, with the Cabinet Office immediately trying to take the opportunity to strengthen Radcliffe's recommendations by making them more restrictive on Ministers than Radcliffe intended. In February 1976 the Cabinet Secretary sent the Prime Minister a proposed 'Declaration on Ministerial Obligations in relation to Memoirs'. He suggested that it need not be discussed collectively by Ministers but should be sent to each of them individually with the Prime Minister's instruction to sign and return immediately. This was a characteristic Whitehall 'bounce' which I strongly advised the Prime Minister to resist. In fact, Radcliffe had stated that a Minister 'on taking office' should have 'his attention drawn' to the Radcliffe recommendations and be 'asked', rather than be required, to sign a separate document simply stating that his attention had indeed been drawn to the guidelines. The Cabinet Secretary wanted Ministers already in office to sign a Declaration agreeing to obey Radcliffe (rather than just indicating that their attention had been drawn to the document). The issue had been briefly discussed at a special MISC Cabinet Committee in January. The minutes of that Committee said, surprisingly, that Ministers there agreed to sign the Radcliffe declaration, but in fact I was a witness to the fact that they had done no such thing and indeed several of them complained to me about this afterwards. Presumably the Cabinet Office secretaries taking the minutes of this meeting accidentally had a momentary hearing aberration. Indeed, the Home Secretary, Roy Jenkins, had specifically stated in the Committee that nobody should be asked to sign until there had been a chance for a full ministerial discussion. However, the subsequent full Cabinet meeting made no reference to signing the Declaration and anyway the matter was decided by a separate *force majeure*, less tricky than the Cabinet Secretary's curved ball but more effective: several senior Ministers, including Roy Jenkins, Michael Foot, Tony Crosland, Tony Benn, Peter Shore and Barbara Castle, simply refused to sign any such declaration. Mr Wilson seemed content with this situation and at the end of March 1976 wrote to the Cabinet Secretary (through his Principal Private Secretary) saying that he thought it would be unrealistic to ask his successor to request that members of the new Cabinet sign a Radcliffe Declaration. Mr Wilson's clear view was that Ministers should read Radcliffe, but that they should take their own personal decision to publish any memoirs whenever they chose, although they should consult the Cabinet Secretary if their writings raised problems in the three sensitive areas mentioned by Radcliffe – national security, international relations and confidential relationships. But the final decision should be in the hands of the author rather than the Cabinet Secretary. Mr Wilson went on to say that he saw little point in asking Ministers to sign declarations which were not legally enforceable. Subsequently he and several Ministers published memoirs and reflections on British government with little apparent reference to the Radcliffe guidelines (although without intrusions upon the 'sensitive areas').

Looking back, whether as a politician or as a social scientist, over our attempts to scrutinise and reform the legal, medical and engineering professions, the City, broadcasting, and the relationship of the law to publishing (as well as the activities of the press and the review of the gambling laws which were also subject to Commissions of Enquiry), it is difficult to claim much evidence of success. Perhaps our ambitions were ill-founded or impossible. It might also be concluded that Royal Commissions and other such committees of enquiry are an imperfect vehicle of reform. As often as not, one consequence of setting up a commission is to delay the progress of any reforms already under way (although it must be said that there were not many of those within the legal and the engineering professions or the BBC). The committee members themselves are usually selected on a basis which inhibits radical recommendations, with a predominance of 'the great and the good', sound men who have established their reputations through maintaining the status quo and who are therefore acceptable to the Whitehall mandarins who recommend commission members. In addition to the 'sound men' are included the representatives of the existing vested interests (including the trade unions, who are often more conservative than anybody) and usually a 'token' woman, who only remains on the approved token list if she proves amenable to conventional Whitehall wisdom.

Given the deficiencies of Royal Commissions as instruments for analysing problems and recommending change, it is not surprising that they are less used today than in the 1960s and 1970s . However, nothing better has yet been invented and we still need some form of rigorous non-partisan analysis of complex social problems. It was with this in mind that in 1975–7 I participated in discussions initiated by the Ford Foundation to establish an Institute of Policy Research – which came to be known as first the 'British' and then the 'European Brookings', because of its affinities with the famous Washington policy research institute. With the objective of promoting research into problems currently facing the British and European Governments, its staff would include people from government and business and it would aim to be an interface between ideas, the practical world and public decision-makers. It would have been an ideal body to analyse the economic crisis of stagflation which afflicted Britain (and elsewhere) after the oil price shocks of 1973 and 1979.

The initial intention was to establish this institute as a 'British Brookings' in London. The Ford Foundation offered several million pounds and the Social Science Research Council responded quickly with an allocation of £2 million over ten years to support the project. However, the project ran into infuriating, if predictable, problems. It was opposed by existing London research institutes who feared (with reason and good cause) that it would attract attention and funds away from them. It was also opposed by existing social science departments in universities because it would allegedly take public policy analysis away from them – even though they were for the most part woefully failing to carry out or support serious research of this kind. In fact the project would have injected large funds and stimulus into social research at a time when the traditional financial taps were being turned off. However, that prospect did not influence the British research establishment which preferred to continue swimming in a shallow pool rather than allowing big new competition. The proposal was rejected and the Ford Foundation was told to take its millions elsewhere, which it did – to Europe.

A series of high-level meetings were held in Europe, and by 1977 it was finally agreed to establish a 'European Brookings'. The European Heads of Government were then approached and asked to give their support. Mr Callaghan responded with great enthusiasm, as did the Head of the Civil Service, Sir Douglas Allen (now Lord Croham), and the Cabinet Secretary, Sir John Hunt. I attended a further series of meetings at which it was decided to include the European Commission among the sponsors, although the proposed Institute was to remain independent of the EEC. To advance the latter objective, and also to meet one of the original British dreams, I proposed that the Institute should be located in London. The French at first objected but subsequently agreed when I proposed that the first Director should be a Frenchman. Whitehall moved quickly to support a London location and produced an impressive list of possible offices. The Germans lacked enthusiasm throughout, but were finally converted with the help of skilful lobbying in Brussels by officials of Roy Jenkins, then the EEC President. Chancellor Schmidt was scheduled to visit Mr Callaghan in the middle of May 1979 and I was informed by a friend in the Bonn Chancellery that a minor item of his agenda was to give his support for a European Brookings based in London. However, a week before the arrival of the German Chancellor, the British general election produced a change of government. It was Mrs Thatcher, not Mr Callaghan, who greeted Chancellor Schmidt only to reveal that she had vetoed the British Brookings on the grounds of public expenditure. Having led our European neighbours into the field of social research, we then led the retreat. It was a sad waste of much hard work and it was also a wrong decision. Mrs Thatcher might well have benefited from independent, high-quality analysis of her domestic economic dilemmas. Certainly Europe would have benefited from independent analysis of the growing crisis in the EEC, especially in the related areas of agricultural support and the EEC budget. However, our hopes and ambitions on this, as was the case with much else during those frustrating years of the late 1970s, were never realised.

6
Irish Questions

Shortly after entering Downing Street in 1974 we tried to come to grips with a problem which I, as a former professional historian, knew in my heart to be insoluble: Ireland. Harold Wilson had radical instincts on the Irish question and nurtured the same ambition to make progress there which had tempted and misled several previous British Prime Ministers. He had established personal contact with David O'Connell and Joe Cahill of the IRA earlier in the 1970s and had taken a constructive attitude towards Mr Heath's commendable efforts to create power-sharing in Northern Ireland through the Sunningdale Agreement. When Labour entered government in 1974 Mr Wilson hoped to build on that approach.

The Prime Minister, Joe Haines (his Press Secretary) and I had several discussions to formulate a progressive policy. One scheme we devised was for an 'Algerian' solution similar to that imposed by de Gaulle. Another was to adopt a modernised 'dominion status' for the Six Counties of Northern Ireland based on similarities with the earlier constitutional position of Canada. Certain aspects of government, such as defence, as well as final sovereignty, would initially lie with Great Britain, but much of the government of the North would be effectively independent, and the ultimate objective in the distant future was to move to full independence (possibly after some further re-drawing of boundaries). I proposed that there should be a Bill of Rights to protect the civil liberties of minorities and an electoral system of proportional representation to assist non-sectarian parties and counter tendencies towards permanent one-party rule. It also seemed sensible to try to involve other interested nations and I wanted the Republic of Ireland, the

United States and hopefully the EEC to form a tripartite agreement to guarantee the upholding of the new constitution as well as to join with Britain in providing massive economic assistance.

Mr Wilson also drafted his own 'Doomsday Scenario' in May 1974 dealing with the possibility of British withdrawal from Northern Ireland. The scheme included the announcement of dominion status, which meant that Ulstermen would remain subjects of the Queen. Sovereignty would be transferred from Westminster and all UK government institutions and functions in Northern Ireland would be placed in the hands of the new constitutional authority. Minority rights would be constitutionally protected, financial aid would taper off over five years, the British military presence be progressively reduced and, finally, there would be a veto on any further constitutional changes for several years. It was a bold and imaginative, if risky, proposal. Mr Wilson seemed almost afraid of its implications and, apart from discussing it with Joe Haines and myself, restricted its circulation to only a few very senior officials.

We realised that these ideas assumed an optimism about Northern Irish attitudes which found little justification in the 400 years of history since the main British colonisation. However, Mr Wilson was so fertile in ideas and expressed such concern to make an effort that an official committee was established in the Cabinet Office to examine the proposals. I was present on the Committee and some very constructive talks took place. However, the whole enterprise was rendered academic by the Protestant Workers' Strike in the spring of 1974. The effect of the strike was to achieve its aim of demolishing the Sunningdale power-sharing approach, and in the process lessened the chances of any more radical progress. The hard-line Protestant bigots had no intention of sharing power, or sharing jobs, and they certainly would have had no time for a new constitution which would give the Catholic Irish community equal rights.

The full story of the Protestant Workers' Strike never became clear to me in Downing Street. It was obviously a serious threat to law, order and stability in the North. In fact, it is always difficult to impose the will of the state on the Protestants in the

North because the forces of law and order in the Six Counties come from the self-same Protestant community and there is a limit to what the Ulster police will do against their religious brethren. Moreover, General King – a moderate and decent soldier – told us in advance that the army lacked the technical expertise to run the Ulster electricity supply. Nevertheless, the Government's capitulation to the strike was suspiciously and unnecessarily quick. At the beginning we held a meeting at Chequers to discuss how to handle the strike. With the Prime Minister were the Northern Ireland Secretary, Merlyn Rees, the Cabinet Secretary (John Hunt), Robert Armstrong and Tom Bridges from the Private Office, the Northern Ireland Executive (Faulkner, Namier and Gerry Fitt), Joe Haines and myself. We decided to stand firm against Protestant intimidation and terrorism, but once we returned to Whitehall the advice flowing in from all sides turned very pessimistic. The message coming to the Prime Minister from the Northern Ireland Office and the Home Office was that all the demands of the strikers must be met as there was no way of opposing them. Even the normally reliable Cabinet Office seemed to lose its nerve. It was as if Whitehall wanted to end the troublesome Heath experiment and return to the tidy if tyrannical rule of Protestant Stormont. Prime Minister Wilson was not at this moment inclined to embark on a more courageous and risky course. He had no majority in Parliament and his first priority was quite rightly to focus attention on Labour's domestic programme in the hope of winning an early second general election. At Whitsun he made a national broadcast in which he referred bitterly to the 'scroungers' in Ulster, an action which did nothing to improve the climate. Unusually, Joe Haines and I were not involved in the speech-writing; it was drafted by the Northern Ireland Office and Mr Wilson himself inserted the reference to scroungers. To remedy the situation, I arranged for my old friend Michael Cudlipp to join Merlyn Rees and supervise the press and publicity, which led to a distinct improvement. Now, however, Ireland was moved to the margins of the political agenda and our little initiative towards dominion status had no chance. But, when I later discussed the Protestant strike with senior military officers from Northern Ireland they expressed sur-

prise at our precipitate surrender and said that the strike could
have been resisted had central government shown the necessary
will.

Labour's two Secretaries of State for Northern Ireland during
1974–9 were unlike one another in style and attitude. Serving
under Harold Wilson was Merlyn Rees, a delightful Welsh Celt,
with a lovely Irish wife, who became fascinated by the situation
in the North. He could describe in detail the characters of all the
main local participants, many of them quite appalling in nature,
and he closely followed Northern Irish social and political
developments. As a veteran of the Second World War, he also
empathised with the military men in this shadowy struggle. His
contributions to the regular Cabinet Committee on Northern
Ireland were colourful, funny, and almost obsessively detailed,
rather in the manner of a railway and steam engine enthusiast.
His problem was that he could not always see the wood for the
trees and at times he seemed more at home when discussing the
latest incident in Crossmaglen than when in charge of a stuffy
Whitehall department. Despite this shortcoming, he was a man
whom it was impossible to dislike.

Roy Mason was a different kettle of fish. A solid, tough,
practical, patriotic, authoritarian Yorkshireman from a working-
class coal-mining background, he was well organised, well
dressed and his contributions to Cabinet were blunt and to the
point. Also a Royal Air Force veteran, he was more military than
the military and appeared to carry their confidence. The
problem was that he also seemed more 'Protestant' than the
'Prods' and but for his accent might have been taken for a classic
Ulsterman. He had little time for fools or romantics – and
clearly many of the Catholic Irish, whom he called 'greens',
came into this category. He ran his department well and was an
appropriate Minister to conduct a 'status quo' policy of restoring
law and order under direct rule. Some of his officials admiringly
referred to him as 'Viceroy' and invoked Carson in comparison.
Mason was not the man to take the broad sweep of Irish history
in order to consider how to make progress out of the terrible
impasse and fundamentally unstable situation in which Britain
found itself while trying to govern the alienated population of
one of its oldest colonies. However, James Callaghan did not

appoint him to do this, and he was an impressive, if over-rigid, man in a no-win situation.

Following the humiliating capitulation to the Protestant violence in 1974, both Mr Wilson and his successor tried not to get too deeply involved in the Irish problem. Our policy became one of consolidation, trying to contain terrorism and just to get through from year to year. The Irish situation regularly appeared on the agenda of the Cabinet Committee on Ireland, but it was mainly a question of reporting information rather than debating issues, and rarely was anything taken higher to Cabinet.

Our policy from 1974–9 was to try to lower the profile of the British military and make greater use of the police in restoring law and order. This tactic enjoyed some success, and the numbers of casualties from terrorism declined significantly after peaking in 1975. The campaign of the security forces was conducted with great skill, and the IRA – who anyway have always shown a marked reluctance to fight in open combat, preferring to shoot unarmed victims in the back or blow them up from a safe distance – were in retreat for most of the period of the Labour Government. However, the logic of the military intervention was to increase the status and impact of direct rule. A kind of downward spiral was created in which the military initiative provoked further IRA military responses and everybody came to depend more and more upon the forces of law and order. The indigenous organs of politics and government in Northern Ireland withered under direct rule and the local Irish Catholic population became ever more alienated. It was a familiar colonial situation in which the military measures necessary in the short term to restore law and order undermined any possibility of long-term political stability. This was reflected in the fact that the Cabinet Committee in Downing Street never after 1974 actually discussed Northern Ireland *policy*: it only discussed law and order.

Although I sometimes objected to the tough, unimaginative rule of Roy Mason after 1976, I had to admit that it was never very clear what would be a better alternative. I preferred a radical policy leading towards the end of British military rule and ultimately to reunification of Ireland if a majority wanted that. But it is always much easier to say things than to carry them out. Most of the people in the Labour party who shared my ultimate objectives in Ireland seemed to have a frighteningly optimistic – or uncaring – view of the possible consequences and to have little knowledge of Irish history. It always seemed to me possible that a British withdrawal might lead to violence and bloodshed much worse than anything experienced in the present war in the North. Nor was it clear whether the Catholic Irish – who in the Labour party are the native 'goodies' oppressed by the colonising Protestant 'baddies' – would necessarily win. Whereas the Protestants have a strong military tradition and can act in a unified way, the Catholic Irish tend to be more factious and not always effective in mobilising themselves. I once saw a top-secret analysis of all the IRA's known bombing attempts on the British mainland. There were far more than the public or the media might imagine – well over 500 in a few years. However, it was difficult to read the factual and detailed description of each murderous mission and retain respect for the IRA as a serious or professional organisation. Had the motives and intended consequences not been so tragic it would have been very funny. Out of over 500 bombing missions, the number that reached the intended destructive conclusion was in low single figures – and half of these blew up the Irish bombers themselves and not their intended English victims. One team of terrorists travelled round and round on the London Under-ground Circle line hoping to go to the terminus and finally, demoralised, left at the first station they recognised and aban-doned their lethal carrier bag outside. It is not clear whether this miserable army, with a tally of victims over the years containing virtually as many Irish women and children as British soldiers, would triumph over the hard men from the disciplined Protes-tant paramilitary organisations. The regular army of the Repub-lic, according to our secret military analysis, would not neces-sarily be decisive, either militarily or politically. Therefore there were and still are arguments for Britain not pulling out of Ireland. However, the only positive reason for staying in which really mattered in Whitehall was defence. The British military have a 'Western approaches' role in NATO. They value the ports, airfields and barracks in the North and fear the consequences of them being in unfriendly hands (Eire's regrettably sympathetic attitude to Nazi Germany during the Second World War understandably still rankles).

The one case for Britain staying in which certainly does not stand up is the ancient Marxist allegation of British 'economic imperialism' in Northern Ireland. The Six Counties are an economic millstone around the neck of the British Treasury. Suspecting this, but wishing to quantify the cost, in 1974 I suggested to the Prime Minister that he ask the Chancellor how much Northern Ireland cost the British taxpayer. At first the Treasury had no ready answer, as it was not a sum which officials there had previously been encouraged to calculate. A very fudged reply was finally delivered jointly by the Treasury and the Northern Ireland Office in January 1976. It showed that the subsidy from Great Britain to Ulster (excluding Defence) had doubled from £200 per head in 1973–4 to £400 per head in 1975–6 and totalled over £600 million (the figure is now nearly three times that). Public expenditure on Ulster was increasing at three times the rate of public expenditure in Britain. The subsidy to the Harland and Wolff shipyard (which had a bad history of discrimination against Catholic workers) was then £74 per man per week. Given this flow of money from the rest of the UK to the Six Counties, it certainly could not be argued that the British were successfully practising economic imperialism.

Nor was I ever fully at ease with the arguments about territorial colonisation. Certainly the Scottish Protestants had brutally taken the land from the Irish centuries ago. Some of their behaviour towards the native population ever since suggested that they were morally unfit to retain it. However, there is a point where the passing of time often legitimises conquest and theft. If this were not the case, it could be argued that most of the English aristocracy should be disinherited. Where should the process of unravelling colonial history end – with Scotland, Wales, Mercia or Wessex? Of course, most of the Irish do not in general talk of throwing the Protestants out. In our 'dominion status' plan described earlier the proposal had specific constitutional safeguards for both communities. However, the more extreme proposals for rapid British withdrawal do run the risk of bloody civil war and the possibility that disinheritance and an

19 Bernard Donoughue with James Margach of the *Sunday Times*.

20 Sir John Hunt, Cabinet Secretary, outside the Cabinet Room at No.10 in 1976.

21 Labour's Front Bench in the House of Commons, November 1976.

22 The Foreign Secretary, David Owen, sharing a joke with Bernard Donoughue at the Labour Party Conference.

23 Health Minister, David Ennals, addressing an angry crowd of hospital workers in September 1977.

24-26 David Piachaud, Gavyn Davies and Andrew Graham – key members of the Downing Street Policy Unit.

27 Bernard Donoughue at his desk in No.10 during the Winter of Discontent.

alien culture would be imposed on the Protestants just as brutally and arbitrarily as they imposed it on the Catholic Irish community in the past.

I still strongly support a British policy of disinvolvement leading to the restoration of indigenous political institutions in the North. Even so those who talk as if this approach is simple and easy are either foolish or wicked. It has to be handled with great care and could go badly wrong. That is why I always understood, although not agreeing with it, the status quo approach of Mr Callaghan and his Secretary of State, Roy Mason. In the end, however, this conservative approach is actually the most risky because it depends upon preserving a fundamentally unstable social and political balance of power in the Six Counties. The situation will have to be encouraged to evolve and a more progressive policy will have to be adopted with the purpose of loosening Britain's ties and reducing its involvement in the North. Such a policy could not ever succeed without the active co-operation of the Republic of Ireland (which is why Mrs Thatcher and the Irish Government are to be congratulated on their efforts to bring the policies of the two nations into closer harmony). Although for this reason the role of the British Foreign Office is very important, in 1974 I was quickly struck by the fact that the Foreign Office was barely involved in Irish issues. This was later corrected and especially under David Owen the Foreign and Commonwealth Office (FCO) played a very helpful part in bringing into the discussions a liberal international dimension which was entirely missing from the narrow contributions of the Home Office and the Northern Ireland Office (which employed very few Catholics at that time).

Although Mr Callaghan's basic approach as Prime Minister was not to open the Irish can of worms, he was actually very knowledgeable about the problem. He had been Home Secretary when the civil rights disorders erupted in 1969 and had supervised the introduction of British troops (to protect the Catholic minority from Protestant violence). His family had a cottage in the south-west of Ireland and he was on good terms with Mr Jack Lynch, the then Irish Premier. Mr Callaghan's apparently negative approach was based on a political calculation that there was more downside than upside in opening up the Irish flanks and that his Government, which for most of his time in office lacked a majority in Parliament, had other, more pressing priorities. He was almost certainly right politically in this. However, it would be wrong to underestimate the importance of the Irish community to the Labour party. Labour has increasingly become the party of the Celtic fringe, based heavily on Scotland, Wales and the Irish immigrant conurbations of Glasgow and Liverpool. In London and Birmingham the Irish communities also dominate certain Labour-held constituencies. In 1978 I made an analysis – based on the previous census – of how many people in the entire population had either been born in the Republic or who had parents born there. My results found that there were nearly 2 million Irish people of voting age, often concentrated in Labour constituencies. In all it seemed that up to thirty seats were strongly influenced by the votes of their Irish constituents and seven seats had a 5–12 per cent presence of Irish inhabitants. I used these figures to try to push the Prime Minister towards a more progressive Irish policy. I also personally maintained regular contact with the Roman Catholic hierarchy, meeting with Bishop Konstant who was acting directly on behalf of Cardinal Hume. However, I must admit that I had very little effect on our policy towards Ireland. The best I could do constructively was to organise, through my close friend in the Irish Dail, Trevor West, the first ever football game held between the British and the Irish Parliaments. (The only political consequence of this was the subsequent rapid removal of the Irish Ambassador, who at the post-match Embassy reception imprudently terminated the supply of drinks with undiplomatic haste.)

On the contrary, Labour soon moved into an open parliamentary alliance with the Ulster Unionists in order to secure our Commons majority over the winter of 1978–9. This was understandable in terms of Westminster politics, but certainly a step in the wrong direction as far as the future of Ireland was concerned. However, after leaving office Mr Callaghan made an impressive speech in which he argued that the previous Northern Ireland policies, including his own, had failed and it was time for more radical solutions, including progress towards an independent Ulster. Mr Callaghan was right: no present or future British Prime Minister with a Parliamentary majority need again capitulate to the Protestant veto or threat of violence. It is greatly to Mrs Thatcher's credit that, so far at least, she has given a courageous lead in this direction. It was a great disappointment that we in the Labour Governments did not do more.

7

Two Years of Stability: Callaghan and Healey in Control, 1977–8

Whether because of the tighter policies which were imposed by the IMF, or simply because the IMF stamp of approval created a climate of confidence, the Labour Government's economic policies seemed to be working better in 1977. The Government's position in Parliament was also much more stable after the pact with the Liberals in March 1977. A joint consultative Committee of the two parties was established to consider all policies coming before the Commons. The Prime Minister and the Chancellor agreed to meet regularly with their opposite numbers, David Steel and John Pardoe. On this basis the Liberals normally supported the Government.

Inflation moved down into single figures for the first time since 1974, public expenditure was actually reduced and sterling was strong. Indeed the new 'economic seminar', a secret high-level committee whose members (including the Chancellor and the Governor of the Bank of England) after the IMF crisis began to meet regularly in Downing Street to discuss monetary issues, was mainly concerned with how to hold sterling down. The Prime Minister especially was concerned to avoid the deflationary pressures and higher unemployment which would follow from a strongly rising currency. However, the Governor of the Bank of England courteously but firmly disagreed with the Prime Minister. He liked a strong sterling, enjoying the counter-inflationary benefits and the inflow to the reserves which actually allowed some debts to be paid off. To this end the Bank maintained a 2 per cent premium on short-term sterling interest rates compared to Euro-Dollar rates. By the

end of July 1977 sterling was rising towards $1·80; early in
September it was still going up and inflows to the reserves were
approaching $1 billion a week, which put pressure on the money
supply. The Prime Minister repeatedly urged the Bank to
reduce interest rates more quickly but the Governor resisted,
preferring to be absolutely certain that the policy would not have
to be reversed and also using the strength of inflows to repay
some debts. The debates on this issue in the 'economic seminar'
were absolutely fascinating.

The 1977 budget suffered some parliamentary embarrass-
ments when critical amendments were passed at the committee
stage. The increases in personal tax allowances and the can-
cellation of our proposed petrol tax increase added about £450
million to the PSBR, but as the Treasury PSBR forecasts had
been deliberately inflated at the time of the IMF crisis in order
to create a greater sense of urgency, there was actually a little
elbow room to accommodate these increases. The real interest
of these alterations lay in the example they gave to the political
problems of budget-making when in a parliamentary minority.

The main problem facing the Government in economical
terms during the first half of 1977 remained the pursuit of its
counter-inflation pay policy. The Treasury wanted a rigid 10
per cent earnings target and this simple, clear approach ultimately succeeded in gaining the Prime Minister's support. None
the less, there was considerable discussion of alternatives among
Ministers. Michael Foot and Albert Booth were closest to the
TUC position and argued for very loose guidelines. They also
wanted to make major concessions on taxes and on low pay to
win over trade union support. However, Mr Callaghan never
really believed that the unions would deliver more in return for
these concessions, even though they would happily accept them.
Roy Hattersley, who was rapidly making a mark in Cabinet, put
forward interesting compromise proposals. He wanted to establish a national wage bill target of 10 per cent but to allow some
flexibility around that figure, especially where special circumstances of productivity or pay anomalies were involved. The
Treasury invited the Policy Unit to participate in the drafting of
the summer White Paper on Pay and Gavyn Davies and I tried
to incorporate in the drafting some of the Hattersley dimension.

During the autumn of 1977 the Prime Minister and the Policy Unit looked to ways of trying to stimulate the economy without losing the hard-won advantages recently gained in the battle against inflation. The economic prospect was of a combination of rising unemployment, inflation just in single figures, a balance of payments surplus of about £2 billion in 1978, and a PSBR falling slightly to £8·5 billion by the next year. This suggested that a relaxation in the Government's fiscal position was both desirable and possible. We considered the possibility of a reflationary autumn budget – although it could not contain direct tax cuts as the Inland Revenue staff were refusing to take on any extra work. This was particularly disappointing to the Prime Minister who was personally very committed to introducing a reduced rate tax band of 15 or 20 per cent, so that the first portion of taxable income was taxed at a lower rate. The Policy Unit did a great deal of work on the details and implications of a reduced rate band (which the Chancellor did subsequently implement). I sympathised with Mr Callaghan's desire to introduce an intermediate step, especially when the basic rate was as high as 33 to 35 per cent as it then was. However, my own personal priorities were always to raise tax allowances in order to remove the maximum number of people from the bottom of the tax net and to increase child benefits, the latter of which was the most effective way of helping the really poor in our society.

However, our optimism about giving the economy a reflationary boost in the autumn of 1977 soon suffered a setback on the monetary front. The Bank of England communicated to Downing Street that it was seriously worried about firstly, the continuing sterling inflows, which threatened the IMF 9 to 13 per cent monetary targets for 1977–8, secondly, about the rapid increase in bank lending to the private sector, and thirdly, about the difficulties being experienced in selling gilts. The Bank's reaction was to propose a sharp increase in interest rates which promised to mitigate the second and third problems but to aggravate the first by attracting further sterling inflows. A series of 'economic seminars' were held in Downing Street during October and November 1977 at which the Prime Minister, the Chancellor and the Governor thrashed out these dilemmas. Everyone agreed that it was now necessary to deter massive inflows into sterling because of their monetary consequences and their interest costs (even the Governor, now he had over $20 billion in the reserves, was keen to call a halt). However, the Bank's policy of raising interest rates and allowing sterling to float upwards did not seem ideal to us, both because of its deflationary effect on the economy and because it might perversely encourage even greater inflows. We therefore explored the possibilities of direct controls on the banking system and selling alternatives to conventional fixed interest gilts. We also agreed with Harold Lever that it would be preferable to take a relaxed view of modest breaches in the 13 per cent monetary targets than to hit the economy with devastatingly high interest rates. At a final discussion in Downing Street in late November the Governor won his battle. It was conceded that interest rates should rise by 2 to 7 per cent. This increased the debt-servicing costs of the Government by about £500 million in a full year and so reduced by a quarter the Chancellor's scope for tax cuts in the coming budget. However, in real terms it was still a negative rate of interest and very low by the standards later established by Mrs Thatcher.

Going into 1978 we had to bear in mind that this might be an election year. Therefore from Downing Street we fought a battle to loosen the constraints and targets set out in the annual Letter of Intent to the IMF. We were successful in excluding references to tight control of the money supply but failed to remove references to a limit of £8·6 billion for the PSBR. The latter threatened to restrict our budgetary scope for pre-election generosity but the Treasury insisted on keeping it, understandably worried that the markets would take fright and lose confidence in our commitment to defeat inflation. Instead the Prime Minister warned that he might want to repay the IMF loans and so gain freedom later in the year.

Just before Christmas 1977 I sent Mr Callaghan a long Policy Unit 'green paper' for his recess reading. It analysed the prospects for the economy over the next eighteen months in order to try to identify the most favourable time to hold a general election. Of course we could not be absolutely confident of controlling our own destiny. In the New Year of 1978 we were in an overall parliamentary minority of fourteen. However, with the help of the Lib-Lab pact and some support from the Northern Irish we could hope to defeat the Conservatives in the Commons even if they were joined in the lobbies by the Welsh and Scottish Nationalists (which was unlikely while devolution was alive). Our conclusion was that the autumn of 1978 would be the most propitious time because the economy would be then at its most supportive. Price inflation should then be in single figures, GDP growth would be at around 2·5 to 3 per cent, real take-home pay would be rising strongly at 6 per cent, and unemployment would be steady at below 1·5 million (6 per cent). Looking ahead into 1979 our forecasts naturally grew less secure. None the less, it seemed likely that prices would be pushed up again by the 15 per cent earnings increase in the current pay round. The balance of payments and sterling were also expected then to run into more difficult waters. Above all, we could not be certain of holding the pay policy together beyond this 1977–8 round. Therefore we concluded that economic factors pointed to an election in the autumn of 1978. We recommended November rather than October because then 12 million people would receive their pension and social security upratings and 7 million families would gain from any increase in child benefits.

With the electoral timing in mind, the 1978 budget would clearly be of crucial importance. Although the Treasury figures pointed to a possible reflation of £2 billion, it was a delicately balanced decision. If there was to be an autumn election it was desirable to be as generous as possible. However, there was not a great deal to give away and it would be politically imprudent to dissipate everything now, in case the election was delayed until the spring of 1979. Moreover, there was an economic risk in being over-generous, as if market confidence was shaken the Government's recently acquired image of economic competence would be damaged. Within any given amount of financial stimulus there were also difficult choices to be made between tax cuts or greater public expenditure; the opinion polls demonstrated the greater popularity of the former, while Labour spending Ministers always preferred the latter. Mr Callaghan characteristically approached these issues with careful political preparation. Again showing his preference for involving ministerial colleagues, he summoned a special Cabinet at Chequers in late February 1978 to discuss economic strategy. He also had several private meetings with the Chancellor in the Downing Street study to discuss the shape of the budget which finally provided an extra stimulus of less than £1 billion on top of the £1.25 billion necessary to offset the fiscal drag effects of inflation. The emphasis was on higher tax allowances and the reduced rate band for which the Prime Minister had long pressed. Public expenditure remained tightly constrained and there seemed little scope for a big boost in child benefits, to which I was personally very committed. It was hardly a give-away budget to bribe an autumn electorate. Even so the City was sceptical, believing that the fiscal stance seemed too loose to be compatible with the kind of tight monetary targets to which the Government was now dedicated. There was a run on sterling in the spring, but fortunately that nervousness passed.

One aspect of this withdrawal of confidence was the drying up of gilt sales. This had been a recurrent experience under Labour Governments and had led to accusations of politically inspired 'gilt-strikes' by the Tory City. In fact it was nothing of the sort. The system of 'tap' sales was always likely to produce such a 'drying up' periodically. This tendency became more acute under the new method of explicit monetary targets, which inevitably produced instability in the interest rate. The City was interested only in profits and naturally declined to buy gilts at times when the published monetary statistics suggested that interest rates would soon have to be raised. Investors were not being unpatriotic or anti-socialist, but were simply exercising their right not to buy on the expectation of making a quick loss.

The Policy Unit conducted long discussions on how to produce a more even flow of gilt sales and I put some suggestions to the Prime Minister in June 1978. These included variable-rate stocks with convertibility, indexed-linked bonds, and the encouragement by tax changes of unit trust participation in the gilt market. We also recommended the introduction of a tender system to replace the traditional poker game between the Government broker and the institutions. Mr Callaghan presented our paper to the Chancellor and some of these reforms were later introduced. The Treasury was sympathetic but the

Bank of England was at first extremely hostile. However, the Prime Minister followed our suggestion of setting up a working group to look into ways of improving the operation of the gilt market. The working party's interim report in the late summer favoured the early introduction of a new convertible stock. However, this (and the final report in November) rejected most of our long-term suggestions – including indexed-linked gilts and tender selling – on the basis that the present system worked successfully and that the markets would be upset if these arrangements were disturbed. It was clear that the Bank considered its own mode of working both to be perfect and nobody else's business. None the less, in time the pressure of events forced some of the innovations which we proposed.

While the Labour Government's broad economic strategy experienced its ups and downs – with the years 1977–8 being a relatively successful period – there was one economic area where the gloom steadily grew worse: unemployment. The official number of unemployed in 1974 when we took office was 528,000. To a generation which had grown up on full employment that seemed a worryingly high figure. We believed that our economic policies, based upon higher economic activity in the private sector and higher expenditure in the public sector, would soon see that figure down well below 0.5 million. However, the full deflationary impact of the 1973 oil-price shock was yet to come. By 1976 the number of people out of work was 1.25 million. It then stabilised during the good years of 1977–8 and in 1979 was (at 1,235,000) actually down a little below the 1976 figure. However, it still seemed to us that to have 1.25 million people unemployed was unacceptable. We did not even imagine that in another five years under a Conservative government that total would tragically have nearly trebled.

A great deal of time and effort was devoted in Downing Street to thinking and planning how to reduce unemployment. Unfortunately little could be done because alongside the scourge of unemployment ran the scourge of inflation, which by 1975 had rocketed to nearly 30 per cent, was still in high double figures through 1976 and 1977, and only just slipped into single figures in the summer of 1978. Inflation was itself causing unemployment by rendering British exports uncompetitive. The scourge had to be conquered, yet the conventional means of attacking inflation, through the rigorous techniques of tight money controls and cutting public expenditure which were modestly adopted in 1976, themselves added to unemployment. It was for this reason that these Labour Governments put so much emphasis on incomes policy as a preferred alternative to massive monetary deflation of the kind later adopted by Mrs Thatcher with such a devastating effect on the unemployment figures. Labour could not avoid taking counter-inflation measures and these inevitably made unemployment worse. However, in the light of later experience it might be argued that a combination of 10 per cent inflation and 1.25 million unemployed (which was the broad situation when Labour left office in 1979) was not necessarily worse than the situation of 4 per cent inflation and (on today's statistically comparable figures) nearly 4 million unemployed seven years later. Indeed, had the trade unions acted more in their own interests in 1978–9, instead of bringing about the excesses of the Winter of Discontent, the 1979 Labour figure would have been notably better. However, it must be said that none of these unemployment levels should be acceptable in an efficient and compassionate society.

Mr Callaghan was from the beginning very concerned about the unemployment figures and looked for ways to improve them. He was aware that we had entered a new and quite different phase of economic life in the Western world. As he stated in his courageous and commendably honest speech to the 1976 Labour Conference, it was no longer possible for the Government simply to put its foot on the economic accelerator and spend its way out of unemployment. The world of 'stagflation' did not respond to old-fashioned Keynesian remedies. In the hope of improving our theoretical understanding of the economic problems facing us, I arranged for seven distinguished economists from the London School of Economics to come into No. 10 one afternoon in January 1977 to talk with the Prime Minister. My proposed structure for the discussion was that we should first establish and define the different kinds of unemployment; then we should discuss some current theories; and finally consider some possible solutions to unemployment. It was pleasant for me to see again from my happy years of teaching at the LSE old friends and colleagues such as David Hendry, Richard Layard, Marcus Miller and Steve Nickell, as well as such internationally weighty economists as Professors Sargan and Sen. However, the session was not as fruitful as I had hoped. Mr Callaghan asked all the questions from the brief which Gavyn Davies and I had produced for him, along with several of his own. Was there anything new in the development of UK unemployment since 1973 which could not be explained by conventional demand deficiency? Why had the number of existing jobs fallen by so little (185,000) while unemployment had risen by nearly 700,000? Was female participation the main cause of the increase in the working population and would this trend continue for long? If a deficiency of demand was the main explanation of unemployment, why had the latter reached ever higher cyclical peaks each year since 1950? Did improved social security payments, or greater productivity, or deeper structural changes in industry have a major role to play in solving the problem? Would higher capital investment, to which the Labour Government was in principle committed, create more jobs or more unemployed? We wanted to know whether conventional reflation would be sufficient – or even possible – in the current inflationary climate. Would a siege economy of import controls really save jobs? What was the scope for increasing the Government's job creation schemes and employment subsidies (an area in which Richard Layard was the leading expert)? We covered the field, but somehow we did not get anywhere. We were all aware that there was part of the unemployment problem which we did not understand – and the part which we did understand we could do little about. However, for us in No. 10 at least, the discussion helped to clear our minds.

It certainly helped my contributions to a high-level Cabinet Office Committee on Unemployment which the Prime Minister had established at that time with Sir John Hunt acting as a very positive Chairman. The Committee's final report was an excellent survey of the problem, although its proposals for action were inevitably limited by the financial constraints on the Government and the Treasury was naturally very nervous about the potential implications for public expenditure. Unemployment, although a matter of great public concern north of

Watford, had not yet touched Great George Street. (As an example, the long Treasury paper on 'The Economic Outlook to Mid-1979', written in April 1978, made no mention of unemployment.) Actually, different parts of Whitehall adopted varied attitudes to unemployment according to their departmental traditions. The Department of Industry favoured direct subsidies to the private sector, the Department of the Environment preferred direct subsidies to the public sector, whereas the Department of Trade was mainly concerned to resist the encroachment of protectionism. The CPRS produced a report in 1978 calling for traditional Keynesian reflation. The Department of Employment, being closest to the trade unions, showed most consistent concern. Its approach, first under Michael Foot and then Albert Booth, was to devise special employment measures covering job creation, job subsidies, work experience programmes and extra training. The Prime Minister gave these schemes his support as the only positive approach possible while large-scale macro-measures to reflate the whole economy were ruled out by the prime need to conquer inflation. (Mr Callaghan made great play with these micro-measures when making unemployment the main theme of the 1977 world economic summit.) However, there was recurrent confusion about who was actually in charge of these employment programmes. One thrust came from the Manpower Services Commission, for which Booth had ministerial responsibilities, and another through a special Cabinet Committee (GEN 27) chaired by Shirley Williams as Secretary of State for Education. (Shirley was much more positive than her officials in this enterprise.) None the less, considerable progress was made from 1977–8, at least in the field of youth unemployment, where some 120,000 young people were kept off the dole. On the terrible problem of the long-term unemployed, in 1978 Gavyn Davies put to the Prime Minister, and subsequently to an official committee, a radical proposal to guarantee a job or a training post to every one of the long-term unemployed. To me this seemed a dramatically attractive scheme; it was intrinsically desirable and would also have proved invaluable in the coming election. The *net* cost of reducing the then total of 330,000 long-term unemployed by two-thirds would have been less than £200 million a year; for such a worthy objective that seemed a modest price. However, it was too high a cost for the Treasury, and Ministers seemed sadly apathetic towards the idea. As with the sale of council housing, this scheme was left for the Conservatives later to adopt in a modified form at a time when the social cancer of long-term unemployment was devastatingly more serious.

The Government also hoped to improve the working of the real economy and mitigate unemployment through its industrial regeneration policies. These had been set out in the White Paper issued by the Department of Industry (and rewritten by the Policy Unit) in 1974. Subsequently the Government's attention and energies were diverted and almost wholly concentrated on its counter-inflation policies. However, the Cabinet Committee on Industry continued to meet and, using the National Economic Development Office (NEDO) as a forum to discuss these questions with management and the trade unions, an interventionist 'Industrial Strategy' was slowly formulated. Under the auspices of NEDO, working parties were formed for each industrial sector, each containing a dozen or so members from both sides of a particular industry. These reported on their individual problems and bottlenecks and made recommendations on how to improve productivity and competitiveness. In some cases little emerged except endless debates and reports, but some of the working parties made constructive progress. The fact that both sides of industry were sitting down together to discuss ways of improving efficiency was in itself progress. It was easy to laugh at this interventionist approach at the time and the Conservative party was scornful of it then and later. However, this approach was probably no worse than the subsequent policies which laid British industry to waste; many of these working parties would now no longer have an industrial sector to represent.

Although the Labour party was in 1974 still committed in principle to extending public ownership, in practice its traditional approach of state nationalisation was almost abandoned by Mr Wilson and Mr Callaghan. It was pursued in the shipyards – to the great relief of the private owners who, while remaining the staunchest supporters of the Tory party and denouncing public ownership in all its forms, were in nearly every case ready to take the Labour Government's cash for their near bankrupt yards. Increasingly, the Government confined its public enterprise activities to the National Enterprise Board which recruited able managers and acted as the agency for state intervention in such areas as micro-chip development, where private industry was proving slow to invest. The NEB also became a convenient casualty ward for firms which the Government wished to rescue from bankruptcy. It had more success than it was credited with by a biased media, but the scale of its activities was small and it could scarcely be considered as the new frontier of a socialist industrial policy.

High hopes were also briefly entertained that British industry might be regenerated by the introduction of greater industrial democracy. The argument was that if British employees became more involved in the decisions affecting their working lives they would work harder and show more commitment to the success of their firms. As a concept it had then, and still retains, great validity but unfortunately we were not able to advance it far in practical terms. Under the historian Alan Bullock a Royal Commission was set up, the report of which made a number of sensible radical proposals which would give a right to workers' representation on company boards provided that at least one-third of all the eligible workers had voted in favour. However, the weakness of the Commission was that it was dominated by trade union representatives which resulted in proposals which saw the existing trade union structure as the only form of employee representation. It argued for greater trade union representation rather than employee representation and, given the undemocratic nature and processes of many trade unions, it would undoubtedly have led to undemocratic industrial democracy. Given the unpopularity of all trade unions at that time, it meant that there was precious little chance of a majority of workers, let alone of management, supporting the reforms. Certainly some of the opposition to industrial democracy which was expressed in Whitehall at the time was foolish and reactionary – many senior officials were shocked at the very idea of workers participating in management decisions and seemed totally unaware that in some other countries this 'extremism' was both familiar and helpful. However, the narrow base of the proposals, weighted as they were towards the unions, made it difficult to support and easy to oppose them. Sadly, what might have been a major social advance and contribution to the greater efficiency of British industry ran, via endless bickering in committee, into the political sand.

Amid the encircling economic gloom of the mid 1970s the one strong gleam of hopeful light was North Sea oil. Everyone in Government was aware that the benefits, however they were channelled, could be enormous. The only question then was whether the oil would arrive in time to help this Labour Government. We often said that whoever won the coming 1978–9 general election was bound to float through the following election on the oil revenues. For the first time in decades there should be no question of balance of payments deficits, or, we optimistically imagined, of Public Sector Borrowing Requirements. We did not conceive that a future Government would allow the oil to push up sterling to ludicrous levels or would spend so much of the oil proceeds on unemployment pay. We were naïve, but we had no experience of an oil economy or a petrocurrency.

Although North Sea oil would not arrive onshore in significant quantities until after the latest possible election date, the first flow began shortly after we took office and the Government began early to plan that its benefits should go to the British people rather than to overseas oil companies. The British National Oil Corporation was established to secure ultimate British control of the commodity and a tax regime was devised which gave sufficient incentive to the oil companies to continue exploration but ensured that significant revenues would come to the Government. (We were conscious of the appalling historic record of the oil giants in exploiting oil wells in poorer countries, leaving no benefits at all to the local population and equally paying very little tax in their home countries.) In these arrangements several Ministers played a notable part: first Eric Varley and then Tony Benn as Secretaries of State for Energy, assisted by the wily machinations and passionate patriotism of Thomas Balogh, the Oxford economist, and by the financial genius of Harold Lever (Chancellor of the Duchy of Lancaster). Tony Benn quickly fell out with his officials at the Department of

Energy and sometimes Cabinet was openly presented with two points of view, that of the Department and that of the Secretary of State. However, I thought that Tony's contributions on North Sea oil were often excellent and at times prevented the Government from being taken for a ride.

By late 1977 the question of how best to exploit the expected benefits of North Sea oil was being actively discussed. The Liaison Committee, consisting of senior figures from the Labour party and the TUC, had asked for papers and clearly it would become an issue at the next party conference. Tony Benn produced a document called 'How Should Britain Spend its North Sea Revenues?' and the Treasury replied with a draft green paper on the same theme. Mr Callaghan became worried that the matter would get out of hand and lead to public squabbling, thus giving the Government some political disadvantages of North Sea oil long before we enjoyed the economic benefits. He therefore asked me to produce a paper on the broad policy issues arising in connection with oil, setting out the questions and the various choices, including the relevant facts and figures. The Policy Unit did this in as non-contentious a way as possible and the paper was put before the Liaison Committee. However, Mr Callaghan decided not to attend this meeting, which cooled and delayed matters a little until the Prime Minister brought the issue back under his control.

The differences of view on how to exploit the oil ran deep in the Cabinet. The Treasury approach was, crudely, to use the oil to swell general Government revenues, to repay debts, to cut taxes and to encourage investment overseas (which has been Mrs Thatcher's basic policy). Mr Benn's approach was to take this unique opportunity to direct investment into the nationalised industries, into the social infrastructure, and into energy conservation and new energy sources. He wanted to use state agencies such as the NEB to invest directly in existing and in new industries and to set up a North Sea Development Fund as the funding agency through which revenues were to be directed to these activities.

Both these approaches had their virtues. The Treasury approach, by reducing debt and increasing income from overseas investment, ensured that the benefits of the North Sea would continue after all the oil had gone. Tony Benn's proposals would have made sure that the revenues were not simply lost in general Government income and frittered away on social security payments, but actually led to visible projects on the ground. However, the disadvantage of this latter dirigiste approach was that on past experience much of the investment would prove wasteful, being directed to where the shop stewards' committees were most vociferous.

The oil battles between Denis Healey and Tony Benn at the end of 1977 were quite savage and the Prime Minister sought to bring the issue back under his central control. He asked the Cabinet Office to draft a White Paper on The Challenge of North Sea Oil and, when that draft proved too anodyne, he asked me and the Policy Unit to redraft it in a more positive vein and with a political dimension. This we did, seeking a compromise between Benn and Healey, although clearly introducing proposals to channel significant revenues into investment in British industry and to greater public investment (which had been totally absent from the original Cabinet Office draft). We supported tax cuts but made no suggestions for cutting debt. We also wanted something added on the need to ensure that oil revenues did not force sterling up to artificial levels, thus destroying Britain's competitiveness. Our major drafting amendments were incorporated in the White Paper, together with many detailed suggestions by the Prime Minister himself, and drafts went to two Cabinets early in 1978. When the White Paper was published in March, in a sense it satisfied nobody completely. It was too general for Tony Benn and many on the left of the party who saw the oil revenues as a godsend to finance their favourite public expenditure projects. The lack of a precise commitment to channel the revenues through a North Sea Oil Fund was obviously a major defeat for them. Even so, the Treasury was worried that it opened the door in principle to pre-empting general Government revenues for particular expenditure purposes – something which both the Treasury and the Inland Revenue viewed as the ultimate sin. In addition, the Treasury obviously wanted to get its own hands on all the revenues. However, the White Paper represented a reasonable compromise solution and it was a basis on which a future

Labour Government might have exploited the revenues in a way distinctly different from what the Treasury wanted and Mrs Thatcher has chosen.

It was also useful politically in holding the Cabinet together around a consensus view, which may not have satisfied anybody very much but left nobody so angry that he or she was forced to resign. Although he was clearly the most important figure in the development of this policy, Mr Callaghan characteristically involved his conflicting Ministers as much as possible in the debate. When Benn and Healey began by making the running, the Prime Minister pulled the issue back under his control into the central capability of Government. The Treasury draft White Paper was abandoned and, in another example of prime ministerial government, the drafting was finally done by the Prime Minister's own advisers, in the Policy Unit and in the Cabinet Office. In the end, of course, it did not make much difference. Mr Callaghan's Government was no longer in office when the oil really began to flow, by which time the Treasury had had its way. None the less, we were right to try to plan in advance for a different eventuality.

8

The 5 per cent Pay Policy and the Non-Election of September 1978

As we reassembled in No. 10 after the August holiday in 1978 we were aware that the main decision ahead of the Prime Minister was whether to hold a general election immediately that autumn; and that the main problem facing the Government was the rapid disintegration of its voluntary pay policy. The two concerns were politically interlinked.

The question of what norm to establish for the 1978–9 pay round had been under discussion since the spring. The Prime Minister told me after the 1978 budget that his preference was for a zero norm on pay increases in 1978–9, although he expected to have to compromise at around 5 per cent. As far as he was concerned defeating inflation was the first priority as he believed it was necessary to defeat inflation in order to defeat unemployment. The question of the next pay round was placed on the Cabinet Committee agenda and the Treasury papers submitted to the Committee mentioned a target of 4–5 per cent. After discussion Ministers finally decided on 5 per cent and this was publicly affirmed in the Treasury White Paper in July.

It is very easy with hindsight to criticise the 1978–9 5 per cent pay norm. After its failure most people, including the whole of the media, recalled their initial total confidence that it would fail. At the time, however, nobody seriously argued against the basic thinking behind the policy that 5 per cent was the highest figure on basic pay settlements which would enable inflation to be kept down to the then current level of around 8 per cent. Larger pay settlements would mean that the rate of inflation would rise, which would be damaging in the coming election as

154

the Government's main claim to success was that it had definitely controlled inflation. Some upward drift in earnings was inevitable, but, provided pay increases were partly accompanied by increases in productivity and did not push inflation into double figures, the Government could live with it. Double-figure inflation was bound to be politically damaging, both because 10 per cent is psychologically far greater than ten times 1 per cent, and because it would take inflation above the level inherited from Mr Heath. The most acute danger lay in the public service sector where in the 1970s pay increases were almost never accompanied by higher productivity (a concept then apparently unknown to most public sector managers or workers).

The Government's strategy, therefore, was to hold inflation in single figures during the election year 1978–9 and, as we have seen, this required basic pay rises of not more than 5 per cent together with modest earnings drift. On that basis the 5 per cent norm could and can be totally defended in principle; indeed, critics never then or subsequently discussed it in those terms. Left-wing critics simply opposed any restraint on pay, yet could provide no alternative policy for containing inflation. They accepted inflation without understanding its implictions for unemployment. Among right-wing critics, Mrs Thatcher did at least then argue an alternative policy for controlling inflation and she has since put it into force. Mr Callaghan and his Government were aware of this alternative policy but preferred not to introduce it at the expense of 3–4 million unemployed. The only economic strategy which was acceptable to a democratic socialist Labour government, and which in the prevailing economic situation did not involve either the high inflation consequences of left-wing policies or the high unemployment consequences of right-wing policies, was a pay policy with a low norm. In the event, however, the policy proved impractical because the Government and the trade unions could not deliver the necessary low norm of around 5 per cent, a political failure for which Mr Callaghan and his Government paid the price at the next election. It was, of course, always on the cards, although it was not inevitable, that they would fail politically to deliver on pay. Despite this, the basis of the economic argument was perfectly respectable and as such it was approved by the Cabinet in mid July 1978.

Discussions on the norms to be established for each pay round since the agreement of the incomes policy in 1975 were held with half a dozen top trade union leaders who had visited the Chancellor for talks during the summer of 1978. The problem of deciding who should be chosen as representatives was resolved by using the six TUC representatives on the National Economic Development Council (NEDC). The TUC officials never formally approved the 5 per cent norm, and at times suggested amending the figure upwards, but they knew that 5 per cent was the objective and they never said no.

It subsequently emerged that a number of these trade unionists had serious doubts about delivering 5 per cent but did not express them loudly to the Chancellor or in public because they believed that there would be an election in the autumn after which, whatever the outcome, the pay situation would be different. On the assumption of an imminent general election it was perfectly reasonable for the trade unionists to appear not to dissent from the counter-inflation White Paper, on the basis that it would not be put to the test. The possibility of an autumn election was therefore already an important political factor in the summer of 1978, confusing the pay policy negotiations and leading different people to enter the pay negotiations on a variety of assumptions. Furthermore, the 5 per cent norm was running into trouble elsewhere. It was frequently denounced and was also voted against at several individual trade union conferences held during the summer. The most devastating defeat was that by the giant Transport and General Workers' Union, whose General Secretary, Jack Jones, had been a co-author of the incomes policy in 1975 and was convinced he could deliver it again. By August the prospects for the Trade Union Congress due to be held at Brighton in the first week of September were growing gloomy. At this point the question of whether Mr Callaghan should call an early general election moved on to centre stage. During the previous twenty-one months since the IMF crisis Labour's economic performance had improved immensely. This was partly because of the tough monetary policy which had been imposed under the auspices of the IMF and which was still intact. It was also because of the dramatic reduction in wages and price inflation which had been achieved since the introduction of the voluntary incomes policy in the summer of 1975. However, that was now under pressure and showing symptoms of disintegration. The choice before Mr Callaghan in the early autumn of 1978 was clear. He could either try to capitalise on his major economic achievements by calling an early election before things went seriously wrong on the wages front, or he could soldier on into the following year with the intention of repairing the pay policy and so demonstrating that inflation could be conquered in the longer term without resorting to mass unemployment. When making his decision the Prime Minister also had to calculate whether he could in fact win an election held in the autumn.

Constitutionally a general election was not necessary until October 1979, but as a minority government Labour would obviously look for an opportunity to go to the country early. During the previous Christmas recess I had written a long strategy 'green' paper for the Prime Minister setting out the options open to him on election timing. My paper concluded that the autumn of 1978 would be the most favourable time for an election; November rather than October because large social security increases in both pensions and the new child benefit scheme were due then and there did not seem to be much point in going to the country before millions of natural Labour supporters had those benefits in their pockets. (The Policy Unit had long fought for improved child benefits in the face of much ministerial and bureaucratic scepticism.) The Prime Minister responded appreciatively but said that he was keeping his options open. He felt, as he explained to me in a subsequent conversation, that members of the public usually need to enjoy several months of higher prosperity before they begin to appreciate it. He believed that the economy would start to pick up in the summer but it might be some time after that before the electorate would respond with a more favourable view of the Government. Mr Callaghan was trying to 'fine-tune' the economic/electoral cycle. He was also aware that Mr Heath had never been forgiven for losing the election when he dissolved his Government early in 1974.

However, Mr Callaghan genuinely kept his options open by beginning to clear the decks in case he decided to call an early election. He held meetings in the spring and summer of 1978 with David Steel, the Liberal leader, and himself suggested that the Liberals should disengage from the Lib-Lab pact. He explained that should there be an election that year it would be to the Liberals' advantage if they detached themselves early and fought as a clearly independent party, instead of breaking away at the last moment solely because of the election. Mr Callaghan always dominated the meetings with David Steel but also demonstrated a sort of paternal concern for the welfare of the young Liberal leader. Of course, Mr Callaghan also had his own interests in mind. He wanted a free hand in drafting the next Queen's Speech in line with a possible Labour manifesto. He certainly did not want to have to draft a bland Queen's Speech in order not to offend the Liberals, find himself beaten on it in Parliament and then have to go to the country fighting on an empty programme (or be in the embarrassing position of having to produce a hurried manifesto very different from the Queen's Speech). Anyway, the Liberals disengaged in July on the assumption that there would be an autumn election, thus terminating a very successful if brief peacetime experiment with a kind of coalition politics. When it emerged that there was not to be an election, both parties faced the next parliamentary session in a weaker position.

Even after the Liberal disengagement it was still not certain whether there was going to be an early election. During the summer the Prime Minister was clearly cogitating about this. Mr Callaghan's habit was not to talk much about whatever was most bothering him. Occasionally he would mention this worrying issue, implying that his preference was inclining in a certain direction, but this was just to provoke a reaction; he was trying the argument out to see what it sounded like. While we could see that he was pondering the election question, we had no idea what he would decide.

He actually continued to prepare for both options until the very last moment. The break with the Liberals had been in preparation for an early election, but he also paved the way in case he should decide to continue into the next session by negotiating the continuing support of the Ulster Unionist Party. The Ulster Unionists had committed themselves to support the Labour Government at the time of the Lib-Lab pact in return for an agreement to set up a Speaker's Conference on increasing the number of Westminster seats given to Ulster, and they did not now withdraw from the pact. Both the Prime Minister and the Northern Ireland Secretary, Roy Mason, held private talks with the Ulster leader, James Molyneaux. One day in late July Mr Callaghan said to me, 'I think it is all right for next year,' which seemed to indicate that a deal had taken place guaranteeing the Government a parliamentary majority through the promised support of the Ulster Unionists. In return a Bill was to be introduced in the next session implementing the recommendation made by the Speaker's Conference that Ulster be given several more seats in the Commons.

This was one of the Government's least attractive commitments. It was wrong tactically because it gave a long-term pledge to the Unionists, whereas they were locked in to support the Government only until the legislation was safely passed. Moreover, as Labour had very few other legislative proposals in the pipeline – and since Roy Mason was distinctly pro-Unionist and keen to deliver the goods – the Ulster Bill went through quickly, buying only a few months of parliamentary support. The Bill was also wrong in principle as far as the long-term future of Britain and Ireland is concerned, because it misled the Unionists into believing that their long-term future rested on the direct link to London. Finally, it was wrong for the Labour party politically, since when those extra seats were delivered to the Unionists they would normally in later years vote with the Conservatives. For all these reasons it is debatable whether a Labour Government should have been rushing this legislation through; it was, however, characteristic of the contribution of the Northern Ireland Office at that time.

The Ulster deal did not mean that the Prime Minister was committed to carrying on without an election; he had simply and prudently given himself that option. Probably he had not yet made up his mind. During August he retired to his Sussex farm, taking with him an admittedly now out-of-date poll carried out by Robert Worcester in May which indicated that Labour was then doing less than averagely well in some of its key marginal seats in England. Mr Callaghan also took *The Times* election books for 1970 and 1974 and apparently attempted some psephological analysis. His studies inclined him against an election and this is when he effectively took his decision to continue into the 1978–9 session. None the less, he continued to make preparations to hold an election, recruiting a journalist (Roger Carroll of the *Sun*) as campaign speech writer and telling him to take leave in September and October.

At the end of August the Prime Minister summoned the Cabinet in order to discuss the timing of an election. It was typical of Mr Callaghan's style (as over the IMF crisis) to consult his Cabinet colleagues and try to carry them with him even though the discussion was only in very general terms. From the written record it appeared that there was a definite majority of Ministers in favour of an election that autumn. However, some advisers, either at that Cabinet meeting or at other times privately to the Prime Minister, expressed reservations. Michael Foot was among those who were most strongly against an autumn election. Merlyn Rees agreed with him, having carried out a survey of the Labour party organisation in August, accurately concluding that it was in a bad way and not ready to fight an election. However, this in itself was not necessarily a reason to avoid an election, as it was unclear whether a more active party organisation of the extreme kind then operating in many constituencies would actually attract or alienate potential Labour voters.

Harold Lever and David Owen also seemed to be against an early election. Denis Healey, who potentially had a lot of influence on this matter, actually remained quite neutral, arguing that the economy would be in a similar condition in the autumn or the following summer. As a general conclusion to the views within the Cabinet, it could be said that, with the exception of Owen, the younger Ministers wanted to fight an election that autumn, whereas the older Ministers preferred to wait. The older advisers may have appeared wiser to a Prime Minister who was himself in the older category. Certainly his closest personal allies in the Government – Rees, Foot and Lever – were against holding an election so soon.

However, the final decision was Mr Callaghan's alone and he revealed it dramatically late in the first week of September. I returned from my annual holiday on Monday 4 September and did not see the Prime Minister in person until later in this fateful week. He had gone to his Sussex farm the previous weekend in order to write his speech for the Trade Union Congress at Brighton on Tuesday 5 September. He refused to take any of his personal staff from No. 10 with him – with the exception of just one civil service Private Secretary. I telephoned to ask if I should join him in Brighton, as I had always previously gone with the Prime Minister to TUC and Labour party Conferences, but he replied in the negative, explaining that he wanted to go to the TUC as a fellow trade unionist rather than as a Prime Minister with a large Downing Street entourage. Therefore none of his closest personal staff – McNally, his Political Adviser, McCaffrey, his Press Officer, or myself as Senior Policy Adviser – actually knew what was going on. Indeed, it was probably the only time during my five years in Downing Street that none of the holders of these three key staff positions was informed by the Prime Minister about a major political decision.

On the afternoon of Monday 4 September (the day before his TUC speech) the Prime Minister telephoned me from the farm and said that he wanted discreet help on an important policy question. He wanted to know which star of the Edwardian music hall had sung the famous song 'There was I waiting at the church'. I said that I thought I knew the answer but wanted first to check it with the Policy Unit's music hall adviser, who was, as well as being Chief Leader Writer of the *Daily Mirror*, Joseph T. Haines. Joe replied that it was Vesta Victoria and I conveyed this information to the Prime Minister, who sang the song to the TUC the next day, to my surprise and disappointment ascribing it to Marie Lloyd. He later apologised and explained that his civil service Private Secretary had strongly advised him that the trade union delegates would not have heard of Vesta Victoria, which illustrates the extent to which the civil service often underestimates the trade unions. Even more important was the extent to which the TUC audience failed to grasp the song's scarcely veiled message which was that Mrs Thatcher would be left waiting a considerable time longer before she would be given the opportunity to cross the threshold into No. 10. Virtually everyone believed that it was still just a matter of days before the Prime Minister would call a general election and that he had not done so at Brighton only because, given the current unpopularity of the trade unions, the TUC was the wrong platform from which to launch it. Mr Callaghan's personal staff knew that he was scheduled to give a nationwide television broadcast on Thursday 7 September and it was assumed that the election announcement would be made then.

The TUC shared this expectation. Six leading trade unionists visited Mr Callaghan at his farm on the Sunday before his speech and, after a hearty meal, came away with the firm impression that he would announce an election on the following Tuesday. His failure to do so made them feel snubbed and almost betrayed as they had in fact stage-managed their Congress as an election launch, working very hard to cover up various disputes within the union movement in order to give the Prime Minister a united front. Mr Callaghan genuinely believed that he had not misled the trade unionists at the farm. He presumably meant to be enigmatic (at which he was normally successful). Those present may well have read into his behaviour what they already thought was going to happen, as was the case with his personal team. However, the trade unionists blamed him and their irritation was important since it clouded their future attitudes to his pay policy.

It was a pity that the Brighton TUC went wrong. The song is a lovely song and Mr Callaghan sang it very well; he often sang songs, including hymns, to himself. He and Walter Mondale, the US Vice-President, sang together one evening at a delightfully informal dinner in Downing Street. As a political ploy, giving a message in a popular code might have worked in many contexts. But on this occasion the trade unionists felt that their Congress had been handled in a flippant way. It was a very rare example of Mr Callaghan not quite getting his political touch right. He normally had a superb feeling for an occasion and often, having gone to a dinner with a prepared speech, he would sense the atmosphere, abandon his set lines and talk brilliantly off the cuff. However, when his usually reliable political radar system let him down at Brighton, the trade unionists certainly felt less obligation to try to deliver his pay policy.

The Prime Minister returned to Downing Street, summoned the Cabinet on Thursday morning and informed Ministers of the decision which he would announce in his television broadcast that evening. No officials were allowed in and I sat waiting in the outside lobby for the duration of the brief meeting. When the Cabinet door swung open Ministers streamed out, looking distracted and puzzled as they headed silently down the corridor towards the front door and out into Downing Street. William Rodgers, an old friend, glared at me and snapped, 'That was the most disastrous Cabinet of this Government.' I still did not know what the Prime Minister's decision was and did not learn until after lunch when a journalist from the *Daily Mirror* came to Downing Street to write a profile of the Prime Minister at the start of the election campaign, only to learn that there was no longer any hurry. Several of the No. 10 staff, including the journalist who had been recruited as campaign speech writer, did not hear that there was to be no election until watching the television broadcast in the evening.

The Downing Street staff were particularly embarrassed by the Prime Minister's decision. McNally and McCaffrey had privately briefed the press on the basis of there being an autumn election. Following this advice, the *Daily Mirror*, Labour's only loyal supporter among British newspapers, ran a front page headline naming 5 October as election day; the paper was naturally very upset at having been apparently, if innocently, misled.

It was a remarkable decision conducted in a remarkable way. Normally I knew virtually everything that was happening at the centre of Government, as did two or three others in the Prime Minister's personal team, and it was a strange experience to be kept so completely in the dark. Undoubtedly a major reason in the Prime Minister's mind was to prevent any prior disclosure to the media; but it was not good for morale in Downing Street. As for the substance of the decision, it is impossible to know with certainty whether Mr Callaghan was right or wrong. Had he called an election in September 1978 he might have lost as badly as he did in 1979 (although he and the Labour Government would at least have avoided the horrors of the Winter of Discontent). However, such evidence as we have suggests that Labour's prospects were reasonably good that autumn. The polls were certainly moving the right way. Having been 4 per cent behind in August, and only 2 per cent behind at the time of Mr Callaghan's decision against an election, Labour moved 7 per cent ahead of the Conservatives in October and then did well in the Berwick and East Lothian by-election. Mr Callaghan was far ahead of Mrs Thatcher in the popularity stakes. It would not have been a bad time for Labour to face the electorate, and probably it would have entailed a less high risk than the chosen course of soldiering on through the winter to fight for an unpopular 5 per cent pay policy.

Perhaps only Mr Callaghan really knows why he decided on the latter option. To those close to him he appeared finally to make up his mind only very late in the day. In August, when he retired to the farm to study Robert Worcester's May poll on the marginals, he had tried to view them in the context of a general election. On or around 17 August, he reached the broad conclusion that Labour might improve on its 1974 Election results but would not secure a clear majority. Therefore, there seemed no convincingly positive reason to dissolve early. Since the objective was to secure a firm majority, it seemed reasonable to wait and hope for a better opportunity, especially as the Ulster Unionists were lined up to support the Government and the electorate was expected to begin to appreciate the improved economic climate. However, even though Mr Callaghan effectively took the decision on 17 August, like any sensible politician he still kept some options open. On the one hand he asked Tom McNally and me to draft the next Queen's Speech on the basis of our continuing into the next parliamentary session; on the other hand he told his Cardiff constituency to print his election leaflets immediately for the coming election and on the final Sunday telephoned the *Mirror* newspaper to ask if its industrial correspondent would be available to help in the imminent election campaign. Even over the final weekend some of the Prime Minister's close family felt that his mind was not yet made up, but that he was inclined to fight and expected to lose.

Certainly he enjoyed the mystery, the drama and especially

misleading the press (whom he held in even greater contempt than did Harold Wilson). In the end, however, he followed the course which had probably been his innermost preference throughout the year. The Worcester polls and the advice of his oldest ministerial colleagues reinforced that view but probably did not create it. On this, as on most issues, James Callaghan took his own line. Perhaps at the age of sixty-five another certain year as Prime Minister seemed more attractive than risking everything for another two or three years if he was lucky. More important was that he deeply wanted to secure real and long-term policy successes before going to the country; and the 5 per cent policy, had it worked, would have given him a major achievement in defeating inflation during 1976–9. Most Prime Ministers do care about what the history books say, at least after they arrive at Downing Street even if they do not worry too much about it before then. One must also beware of using hindsight. Knowing what we know now about the Winter of Discontent, it was clearly electorally fatal for any Prime Minister to enter that period without the heightened power of a new election mandate. However, in August 1978, it was not at all clear what lay ahead. It would have required an extremely pessimistic view of human nature in general, and clinical doubts about the mental stability of large numbers of Labour activists in particular, to imagine that the Labour movement would behave with suicidal lunacy in the nine months ahead, making the defeat of James Callaghan and the election of Mrs Thatcher inevitable in the process. Such cynicism and doubts were subsequently justified by events but the outcome could not possibly have been forecast with confidence in September.

The Prime Minister had grown up in an earlier trade union movement and had great faith in its collective common sense. In Parliament he had secured the support of the Ulster Unionists through the promise of extra seats. He felt that through the promise of devolution he had the Scottish and Welsh National-ists on his side, and he had grown accustomed to the natural sympathy of the Liberals. In these ways he had stitched together a parliamentary survival kit, albeit not a very secure one. To continue in government meant that he might be losing the last chance to choose his own election date, as this rag-bag coalition might soon fall apart. However, he surely did not dream that enemies within the Labour movement would do him far more damage than the enemies without.

Mr Callaghan's decision not to go to the country in October 1978 may have been momentous. Had he fought and won it is possible, having presided over the Conservatives during their third successive electoral defeat, that Mrs Thatcher might have been pushed out from British politics (although it is difficult to believe that the tide of disenchantment with collectivism, the trade unions and the public sector which she reflected would so easily have been pushed aside). More certain is that in avoiding the election Mr Callaghan was faced with a more acute pay policy situation, with many trade union leaders feeling snubbed and irritated. Far worse was the fact that the trade union leaders themselves faced a 5 per cent pay policy with which they were publicly and politically associated but to which they did not feel committed and which they increasingly knew they could not deliver. As far as they were concerned, the 5 per cent was to be a convenient election platform rather than a day-to-day negotiating treadmill. After winning the election it would have been a new game anyway. Instead it was immediately the same old game, except that the Social Contract was crumbling as the Government and the TUC drifted apart.

No sooner was the election buzz over than the unions at British Oxygen and Ford stepped in to demand 15 per cent. In the public sector the unions made even higher claims, backed frequently by summer conference decisions to oppose all pay policy. In the parliamentary session ahead the Labour Government had very little in its policy programme to sweeten its way to election victory. On its side it had devolution, which was unconvincing even to the Scots and Welsh, and the Ulster legislation, which was fundamentally wrong. Labour's only policy of credibility and repute was its counter-inflation policy – and even that was about to fall apart in our hands before the electorate's disgusted eyes.

28 Alan Fisher, the leader of NUPE – which did its best to bring down the Labour government.

29 Moss Evans of the Transport Workers' Union with TUC General Secretary Len Murray emerging from pay crisis discussions in January 1979.

30 *Left* Prime Minister Callaghan with Bernard Donoughue.

31 *Below left* Tom McNally.

32 *Below right* Albert Murray.

33 *Right* James Callaghan with his prices policy supremo Roy Hattersley, April 1979.

34 *Bottom right* The Prime Minister talks to Education Secretary Shirley Williams, April 1979.

35 James Callaghan showing his back to Tony Benn.

9

The Winter of Discontent, 1978–9, and Callaghan's Defeat

The decision not to hold an election in the autumn of 1978 left the Prime Minister's personal staff in Downing Street feeling flat and dismayed. We had mentally adjusted for an electoral battle and we felt the need of a new mandate and the renewed commitment which an election victory brings; indeed, the Prime Minister himself would have benefited enormously from the backing of an election mandate in his struggles with the trade unions over pay policy. In fact, we advisers had virtually ceased thinking of what the Government should actually be doing in the parliamentary year ahead. There were no more major policy commitments to fulfil apart from devolution. While it was clear that the Prime Minister had decided to soldier on, it was not clear what destination he was heading for or for what purpose. It is bad for a government – both in terms of its own internal morale and in terms of the electorate's perception of it – just to seem to be hanging on. I therefore immediately set the Policy Unit to work on thinking of fresh themes and initiatives.

Within a week of his decision not to hold an election that autumn, I recommended to the Prime Minister that he give a series of major speeches on the subjects of unemployment, citizens' rights and responsiblities, housing and especially health and revitalising the National Health Service. The latter seemed a particularly appropriate subject, as all the opinion polls confirmed that it was the area where Labour's policies had the greatest public support. We also suggested that he take up the 'family' theme which overlapped all the particular topics recommended. The Prime Minister responded enthusiastically and we

167

prepared draft speeches for the party conference in October and thereafter. Although this helped to restore his momentum as well as ours, there were problems. Mr Callaghan did not wish to appear to be simply trying to repeat his earlier success with the 'great debate' on education. He was particularly constrained by the fact that any discussion of health, housing and unemployment would rapidly involve considerations of greater public expenditure and the Chancellor did not wish to open those floodgates. There was also a deeper philosophical problem. The Labour party, because of its close ties with the trade union movement, inevitably followed a tendency towards what is often called 'producer socialism' – in other words it naturally supported the producer workers in the welfare state, who were represented by the trade unions, rather than the welfare state's customers who were millions of individual citizens. I also wanted to support the producer, but felt that the balance had shifted too far, to the extent that welfare services and especially local government were increasingly run entirely for the convenience of those who worked in them without concern for the needs of the ordinary citizens (and voters) who paid for them through taxes and tried to use them. This imbalance was wrong in principle and politically damaging, a theme which I tried to write into some of the Prime Minister's speeches, arguing that schools were for children as well as for the NUT, that the NHS was for the sick as well as for health workers, and that public housing was for the homeless as well as for local authority housing departments. However, this tactic upset some people in the Labour party, who either had not come across these thoughts before or who denounced them as 'populism'.

In search of revitalisation before the difficult parliamentary year ahead, I also proposed that the Prime Minister effect a Cabinet reshuffle. I suggested moving David Owen to be in charge of Health and Social Services (which needed his political and administrative drive), Roy Hattersley up to Education, Michael Foot to the Home Office (where his libertarian commitments would be invigorating), Shirley Williams to Employment, John Smith (the most able of the younger Ministers) up to Secretary of State for Scotland, Bill Rodgers to Defence, Denis Howell into the Cabinet as Minister for Transport or as Chief

Whip (his great political talents were never fully used) and Joel Barnett to be Chancellor if Denis Healey agreed to become Foreign Secretary (for which he was superbly equipped). The Prime Minister politely declined, knowing more about politics than I could ever dream to. He shrewdly pointed out that the problem with reshuffles is that the people who are favoured no longer have to behave well in anticipation, while those who are dropped or ignored are made enemies for life! Nevertheless, it did mean that Ministers were left looking tired and sometimes bored in their old jobs. It also meant that three of the outstanding younger members of the Cabinet, Roy Hattersley, John Smith and Bill Rodgers, were unfortunately left in junior positions well below their political capacity.

Whatever our efforts to inject the Government with fresh momentum in various fields of social policy, the Cabinet was inevitably soon totally absorbed in economics and especially incomes policy. In fact, the pay situation deteriorated rapidly in the weeks after Mr Callaghan chose not to hold a general election in October 1978. Several major trade unions – including the giant Transport Workers – had voted against participating in an incomes policy at their annual conferences during the summer. The Government attempted to recover the situation by forging a new pay alliance with the TUC. This new Joint Agreement was intended to lock in the rogue unions, as it would leave them in the position of defying the TUC if they opposed the new incomes policy once it was established.

The Cabinet made many major concessions in order to win TUC support for a fresh round of incomes restraint. Special provisions were made for low-paid workers and to reward productivity. Most important, and worrying because of its long-term impact on inflation, was the fact that the principle of comparability of pay (although not, of course, of work effort) was conceded to the public sector. In view of the transparent fact that if the incomes policy failed Mrs Thatcher would certainly be elected, with all that meant for the pay and employment prospects of trade union members – especially in the public sector – it is remarkable that they needed so much bribery to persuade them not to head for disaster.

The TUC met on 14 November 1978 and in the morning the

Economic Committee discussed the Joint Agreement, which had effectively been drafted for us by the senior TUC representatives in the hope that this would ensure its acceptability. From the Government's point of view it contained the important statement of principle that 'the fundamental objective of economic policy in 1978–9 is to keep the annual rate of inflation at not more than the present level, and indeed to bring it down further ... policies affecting incomes ... must be related to this objective.' The Agreement also kept the TUC in play on the Government's side. To secure these general benefits the Government made some specific concessions. The Agreement did refer to impending price controls, but did not specifically mention a 5 per cent pay limit. It extended pay comparability in the public sector, and did not mention the indirect effect of pay increases on prices in the private sector. These were loopholes which would allow concessions in tricky pay situations, but although they provided the flexibility necessary to the pay policy, they had the potential to undermine its universality and its credibility. The compromises in the Agreement – especially the omission of the 5 per cent figure – were considered necessary by the trade unionist drafters in order to secure TUC support.

The TUC's Economic Committee passed the document without any trouble at that morning session on 14 November and in Downing Street we assumed that we could face the winter with at least the TUC in support. At around teatime I was standing by the Press Association tape machine outside the Private Secretaries' room in No. 10 when the news emerged that the afternoon meeting of the General Council had rejected by one vote the unanimous recommendation of the Economic Committee to approve the new Joint Agreement on pay policy. Two key members of the General Council who were committed to support the motion were absent, one on holiday on the Costa Brava.

This defeat was a major blow to the Prime Minister and his ambitions to continue an anti-inflationary policy during the run-up to the general election. It meant that it was perfectly acceptable for any trade union or its members to oppose the Labour Government's pay policy – because it was now TUC policy not to support it. Had the General Council been constituted of personal representatives of Mrs Thatcher it could not have acted more effectively in the Conservative leader's electoral interests.

The pay situation continued to deteriorate. By December there were strikes threatened by oil-tanker drivers (claiming 30 per cent pay increases), road haulage drivers (claiming 20–30 per cent), local authority manual workers (claiming 40 per cent), British Leyland production workers (claiming 37 per cent), and by water and sewage workers rejecting the 5 per cent policy. There was a curious, feverish madness infecting industrial relations and in some cases unions actually went on strike before their pay claims had been submitted.

I briefed the Prime Minister on the Unit's worries about the weakening of our stance on pay policy. The most recent Cabinet Committee papers (the relevant committee was called EY(P)) had proposed to concede pay comparability throughout the public sector if that was what the respective unions and managements wanted – regardless of whether the Government wanted it or the country could afford it. It was also proposed to make major concessions on low pay to local authority manual workers. I sympathised with the latter idea, although not if it was given away as a gratuitous gesture. The problem was that the Government was in danger of conceding to the unions all the concessions originally contained in the Joint Agreement without receiving anything in return. The Prime Minister responded positively to my worries and on his instructions I wrote to the Chancellor. Denis Healey spoke to me about this; we both agreed that the worst outcome would be to concede comparability to the public sector on an *ad hoc* basis, without having the benefits of agreeing a comprehensive deal on pay restraint. However, in actual fact, this was exactly what was happening. The Cabinet held discussions in which members were tough on general principles, but individual Ministers preferred a quiet life and an easy way out when it came to particular settlements involving their own departments. Many Ministers were in the front line of the battle over public sector pay: Peter Shore with the local authority manual workers and the water workers, David Ennals with the NHS ancillaries, Shirley Williams with the teachers and Fred Peart with the civil servants. In the private sector Bill Rodgers faced the transport drivers and Eric Varley the mutinous workers at Ford and British Leyland. Early in December the Cabinet implicitly abandoned its 5 per cent pay target and agreed that up to 8 per cent could be offered, although this was not announced publicly. Preparations also began to declare a State of Emergency in order to deal with the strike of oil-tanker drivers.

Added to this general undermining of its pay policy, the Government suffered a major blow in the private sector just before Christmas. Ford had settled for 17 per cent and British Oxygen for 10 per cent. With British Leyland facing claims of up to 37 per cent, this was a test for the battery of sanctions which might be used to stiffen the resistance or punish private sector managements inclining to settle at these high levels. However, the legal sanctions supporting pay policy were defeated on a motion in the Commons (when five left-wingers deliberately abstained to assure a majority to Mrs Thatcher). This setback was not a total surprise as the Prime Minister had always assumed that at some point pay policy in the private sector would open up. None the less, it was very damaging to the Government's authority to be defeated in Parliament on a central policy issue.

Things were clearly slipping. By Christmas 1978 the Government had effectively lost control of pay in the private sector, and there were numerous strikes looming in the public sector. As the *Economist* journal said in its headline on 23 December: '15 per cent is the Going Pay Rise'.

The problem for the Government was that 15 per cent represented a total defeat for its main (indeed its only major) current policy objective. While looking into the election year ahead, the defeat on sanctions in the private sector meant that Labour's only continuing policy of constraint applied to the public sector alone, and its policy on incomes was not now greatly different from that of the Conservatives. Before the election Labour desperately needed to reconstruct a credible pay platform to replace the now torpedoed previous policy and which would be distinctive from the Tory policy. I held long meetings of the Policy Unit and sent a brief to Chequers for the

Prime Minister to read and reflect on over the Christmas break.
We suggested that the Government should construct and
announce a new Three-Year Programme on pay policy whereby
there would be pay targets of diminishing numbers over the
following three years with the objective of low single figures by
1982. These targets would be supported and reinforced by
setting tight monetary policy constraints and cash limits. Private
sector settlements were to be limited by using the Price
Commission to apply direct sanctions to individual companies
which breached the pay norm, a measure that would require
legislation. In the public sector a body would be set up to
establish pay comparability with the private sector according to
very strict criteria. This latter proposal had been suggested in a
paper submitted to Downing Street by two Oxford dons (Bill
McCarthy and Hugh Clegg of Nuffield College), and I had not
initially liked the idea because it was so difficult to compare like
with like; it did not seem appropriate to offer the public services
the rewards of the private sector without requiring the risks and
the extra effort. However, it now provided us with a public
sector plank in our attempts to construct a comprehensive
long-term policy, while also offering a bribe which might take
some of the heat out of the immediate crisis in public sector pay
claims.

In the New Year of 1979 Mr Callaghan was scheduled to go
to an economic conference of world leaders in Guadeloupe.
When I returned from spending Christmas at my Suffolk
cottage and dropped in to his study at No. 10 the day before he
left, he was looking very depressed. He said, 'Bernard, it is all
falling apart. I do not trust the Whitehall machine. I think
Ministers and their departments are quietly selling out. We are
going to wake up soon and find that everybody in the public
sector is settling for 20 per cent and the pay policy has been
sunk.' When he asked my views, I said that we must regain the
initiative and I reminded him of the twin proposals in my 'green
paper': to recover control of pay in the private sector by stronger
price sanctions and in the public sector by a pay comparability
unit. Immediately showing enthusiasm, he telephoned Chancellor Healey, and asked him to prepare legislation on prices and a
blueprint for public sector pay comparability. He also suggested

that the Chancellor talk to the TUC about preparing a new Joint Agreement on this basis so that it could form a platform on which the Government and the trade unions could fight the next election together. The Prime Minister then confirmed this new programme in a letter to the Chancellor, sending copies to other relevant Ministers. In the weeks ahead a new pay policy was actually constructed from these components. The 5 per cent norm was effectively, although not publicly, abandoned. Roy Hattersley brought forward to Ministers some suggestions he had previously formulated for revised and more flexible price controls, which allowed employers to pay more than 5 per cent in pay provided that their improved productivity meant they did not have to raise prices above the 5 per cent norm. Proposals for public sector comparability were drafted (although the criteria were not strict enough, in my view). The special problems of low-paid workers were to be met by devising low-pay supplements and the TUC drafted a code to avoid violent picketing. Taken together this package of policies constituted a plausible approach to pay restraint and, indeed, had it been in operation from the start of the pay round it might have helped to avoid some of the problems which arose in the winter. However, amid the appalling industrial chaos prevailing in early 1979 the package seemed to represent irrelevant paper plans blown away in the gusts of trade union anarchy. Despite this sense of hopelessness, the Policy Unit continued to work on refining the new pay policy and the Chancellor argued daily in committee to hold his crumbling fellow Ministers in line.

By the second week of January, when Mr Callaghan stepped bronzed but bemused off the plane from sunny Guadeloupe, apparently (although not in fact) to question whether there was a crisis in frozen Britain, the country was virtually paralysed. The unofficial strike of road haulage drivers was lamely made official by the leaders of the Transport Workers' Union and, deprived of materials, factories were closing down. Mobile pickets were blocking the ports and there was a serious shortage of food and medical supplies – Ministers considered sending tanks into the ICI medical headquarters to retrieve drugs and essential equipment. The strike of water workers had deprived many places in the north-west of England of fresh water since the New Year.

The sewage workers were threatening to join the water workers. The lorry drivers had turned down a 15 per cent offer and were demanding over 20 per cent. The railwaymen had called a national strike because they wanted a 10 per cent bonus on top of their 20 per cent wage demand. The nightly television pictures of violence and the brutal face of trade unionism were doing terrible damage to the Government and to the trade union movement itself. The pickets were ensuring a future victory for Mrs Thatcher.

The oil-tanker drivers were bought off with a 15 per cent settlement in the second week of January, but the idea of declaring a State of Emergency, first planned in relation to the threat from the oil-tanker drivers, was still in the air. The Prime Minister raised the question on several subsequent occasions as a means of reasserting the general authority of the Government and, although other Cabinet Ministers would not give their support, he summoned a special Cabinet in the middle of January to authorise the issuing of a State of Emergency and to approve his appearance on television to announce the measure to the nation. Trade union leaders were called to Downing Street to be informed of the decision immediately after the Cabinet meeting but many Ministers opposed the idea and the plan was shelved, the union leaders being sent away without being told what they had really been summoned for. When Mr Callaghan subsequently proposed calling a State of Emergency to a regular Cabinet, Ministers again lacked the nerve or the will to go down that dramatic path. Actually, there were arguments both ways on this issue. Whereas a State of Emergency would have been appropriate for the oil-tanker drivers strike because only hundreds of drivers were involved and they could be replaced by specially trained army drivers, it could have done little in practical terms to mitigate the effect of tens of thousands of road hauliers who were refusing to transport goods around the country. However, I strongly urged the Prime Minister to call a State of Emergency on political grounds. The Government at that time looked completely impotent and it was necessary to assert some initiative and show some backbone in dealing with the trade unions. After leaving office Mr Callaghan told me that his greatest regret was that he did not overrule his colleagues and declare a State of Emergency. As things were, the Cabinet preferred to capitulate to the road haulage drivers as they had done with the oil-tanker drivers; Ministers formally decided to pay whatever was necessary to buy off the strike. It was decided to allow an offer of 20 per cent and not to apply any of the price code sanctions against the employers.

The second half of January 1979 was the worst period I had experienced in government since 1974; but not in the sense of being stressfully and exhaustingly exciting as were the great crises over pay in 1975 and over the IMF in 1976. This time the situation was full of humiliation and despair. After the capitulation to the road haulage drivers, everyone knew that the 5 per cent norm had been wrecked and indeed that no limit could now be enforced. Some lorry drivers were still on strike, insisting on, and in many cases receiving, more than the 15 per cent agreed offer. The water workers refused 14 per cent with derision and the local authority manual workers responded similarly to an 8 per cent offer. A million and a half public service workers went on strike, closing hospitals, schools and local authority services across the country. The railways came to a halt. As if to cap it all, the worst blizzards for years hit Britain, bringing roads and airports to a standstill; it was difficult to distinguish between the effect of the weather and the effect of the strikes. The TUC, like the Government, was totally impotent before this anarchy.

There was a deathly calm in No. 10, a sort of quiet despair. No papers were being circulated through Whitehall apart from the depressing minutes of the committees bogged down in an ever longer list of pay negotiations. The only major policy proposal for Cabinet that month was a Treasury paper suggesting a twelve months' statutory pay freeze. The Prime Minister told the Treasury not to bother with pursuing it; he knew that he could not get it through Parliament, and probably not even through his own Cabinet.

Ministers were clearly demoralised. Moving among them as they gathered for Cabinet in the hallway outside the Cabinet room, their sense of collective and individual depression was overwhelming. There was none of the usual cheerful buzz and banter. In the committee discussions many of them, especially

Michael Foot, appeared genuinely puzzled. Denis Healey was very tired, his normally strong face puffy and florid. Peter Shore was enigmatic. David Ennals was at times slightly emotional. It was felt that one or two Ministers, particularly Tony Benn and John Silkin, were playing at politics in advance of a future party leadership contest. Others were clearly inhibited by their membership of, and parliamentary sponsorship by, the unions most damagingly involved in the current strikes. This was very apparent in the discussion of using the State of Emergency against the road haulage workers; the Ministers in greatest opposition tended to be those sponsored by the Transport and General Workers' Union. To an involved observer sitting at the end of the Cabinet Committee table, only Roy Hattersley, David Owen, John Smith and Bill Rodgers – significantly the younger members of the Cabinet – appeared determined, tough and clear as to what they thought should be done.

The Prime Minister was for a time worryingly lethargic. He was clearly very tired, both physically and mentally. It was equally clear that he was very unhappy at having to confront the trade unions. His whole career had been built alongside the trade union movement and he seemed to find it quite impossible to fight against it. Although in Parliament and in private to trade union leaders he made good and firm statements of his general intentions, he too often drew back from taking strong specific actions. He was also reluctant to speak out in public, and several tough speeches were drafted but not delivered.

Basically, by late January 1979 the Government had a choice of three options on the pay front. First was a policy of 'calculated capitulation', whereby we could settle the current disputes at whatever level was necessary to restore peace and then hold a quick election to secure a mandate for a tougher programme thereafter. Second, we could make the present policy more flexible by reaching a quick settlement of the disputes which could not be won, at the same time toughening our stance overall by introducing a stricter prices policy and vigorous monetary measures, including a refusal to finance any public sector settlements above 9 per cent and an imposition of expenditure cuts in the services taking increases above that level. The Policy Unit now put forward this approach on the basis that it would preserve the Government's credibility in the pay area, it did not depend upon the support of weak links in the TUC, and it could be sustained until an autumn election if that timetable were politically the most desirable.

The Prime Minister, however, preferred the third option (which was broadly a continuation of the Three-Year Programme that I had put forward to him in the New Year) of going back to the TUC to reach a new Joint Agreement in support of a new pay norm. The TUC leaders were summoned to Downing Street on St Valentine's Day, 14 February. Beforehand the Prime Minister met with the main trade union leaders from the public sector in the hope of settling the current dispute involving the local authority manual workers before the new concordat was announced. He offered them 9 per cent, together with an August payment in advance of the conclusions of the new comparability unit's studies (thus suggesting that comparability was, as I feared, not going to be applied according to very strict criteria). The union leaders viewed this offer favourably but the General Secretary of the National Union of Public Employees (NUPE) (a union whose members behaved viciously throughout the dispute) later found his executive uncooperative. The St Valentine's summit in Downing Street therefore took place against a background of continuing strikes and violence. The TUC representatives sat round the long table in the large State dining-room and the Prime Minister said that unless they could put together a new Joint Agreement within two weeks he would have to legislate a pay freeze. In response the union leaders were disarmingly honest, saying that they could promise him 5 per cent pay settlements in three years' time, but they could not deliver any restraint in the present pay round. Because of this absence of immediate measures, the Agreement made little impact when it was finally announced in late February after long hours of detailed drafting. However, it was important to the Prime Minister and his Cabinet because it symbolised a restoration of the Social Contract between the Government and the trade union movement. As well as stressing the need for harmony between the unions and the Government over pay policy, the Agreement discussed the control of secondary picketing, no-strike agreements in essential services, and postal ballots. As a policy measure, however, it just seemed to disappear in the wind because it had little or no effect on the chaos and violence in the streets outside. It failed because the union leaders sitting round the long table could not deliver the co-operation of their members. As one representative said at the meeting: 'We all agree with what you say, Jim, but there is nothing that we can do about it.'

The Cabinet continued to play around with ever ascending pay norms. Already in January the norm had risen in a series of Cabinet meetings from 5 per cent to 9·5 per cent. Then, when in February David Ennals formally proposed that it should be 15 per cent, this was attacked by Roy Hattersley, David Owen and Bill Rodgers who cut it back to 10 per cent. Really it was not very relevant what figure was arrived at because the norm existed only in Whitehall committee rooms. Outside on the picket lines people were not taking much notice of agreed norms; nor, indeed were some Ministers. The very day after having been held back in Cabinet to a 10 per cent limit, David Ennals and Peter Shore floated the prospect of 15 per cent. This included a 5 per cent advance payment from the still non-existent public sector pay comparability unit which would be reviewing public sector pay increases – which had actually run ahead of the private sector since 1974 – to the striking local authority and health workers who came under the responsibility of their departments. Yet inflation was still currently in single figures and with good prospects for staying that way providing pay awards were constrained. The softness of Ministers and the belief generated that it was always possible to extract from them an even higher offer was one reason why the union activists so often declined to settle. This was confirmed to me in a private meeting I had at the end of February with a senior official of the health union, COHSE. He told me that nobody on his executive ever believed that the last offer from the Secretary of State 'was the last word'. It is therefore hardly surprising that the Prime Minister became increasingly irritated with the weak negotiating tactics of some of his Ministers – although it was perhaps anyway unreasonable to expect politicians to be involved in detailed pay negotiations with trade union officials who had a lifetime's experience as tough negotiators. Mr Callaghan therefore made Roy Hattersley the co-ordinating Minister, effectively a 'pay supremo' presiding over Cabinet colleagues who were nominally his seniors. To his credit, Mr Hattersley performed this task with predictable relish and considerable success.

By this time in late February the union behaviour on the picket lines had become very nasty indeed, and this was quickly reflected in the public opinion polls which showed a strong swing towards supporting firmer action on pay settlements and especially towards support for Mrs Thatcher; indeed it was at this time that Labour decisively lost the next election. The public sector union activists seemed undeterred by this prospect as they perversely worked to destroy the Labour Government and replace it with politicians much less friendly to the public sector. By now the local authority and health workers were hitting the hospitals, picketing the entrances and refusing to allow access to such ambulances as were still running. NUPE publicly and without apology or sign of compassion announced that they would not allow the sick into hospital; an official stood before the television cameras and stated that 'if people died, so be it'. In many places members of this dismal union also refused to allow the dead to be buried. Such actions made the electorate and politicians alike see the public 'service' sector in a new light and the Conservatives jumped to a 20 per cent lead in the opinion polls.

The Treasury began to propose measures to try to correct the damage being done on the wages front; at the present rate inflation would be 11 per cent by the end of 1979 following an 11 per cent increase in the present pay round, and 14 per cent following a 15 per cent pay round, compared to an 8 per cent inflation outcome from our original target of a 5 per cent basic pay and 7 per cent earnings increase. Interest rates were lifted to a 14 per cent crisis level. The Treasury therefore proposed new cash limits along with a package of proposed public expenditure cuts. The problem was that the higher costs of public sector pay meant that the Treasury was now forecasting a 1979–80 Public Sector Borrowing Requirement of around £11 billion compared to an earlier target of £8·5 billion. Substantial tax increases and expenditure cuts were required to bridge that gap – and this at a time shortly before a general election when the Government might hope to be generous. The Prime Minister rejected the cuts package until the forecasts looked more precise, but the pay explosion had badly knocked the hopes for some pre-election sweeteners to encourage the electorate.

By the middle of March the local authority workers had apparently been bought off with an extra £1 a week on top of the previously increased offer. The focus then moved to the nurses (always an emotive issue), to the teachers, and to the heart of the public sector, the civil service itself, the professional body that was supposed to be administering the Government's anti-inflation policy in general and the 5 per cent norm in particular. This fact did not deter the civil servants from making an average 26 per cent claim for themselves and rising to a peak of 48 per cent for some grades; according to these proposals Assistant Secretaries such as myself would be paid more than Cabinet Ministers (and Permanent Secretaries and Deputy Secretaries very much more than the Prime Minister).

These outrageous Whitehall claims were based on the comparability findings of a notorious body called the Civil Service Pay Research Unit, which made its comparisons with the very highest pay in the private sector, made no serious allowance for the major civil service privileges of job security and inflation-linked pensions, and was staffed by people who themselves actually benefited from their own findings. The official committee discussions of this particular pay claim (which also benefited every member participating in it) were very interesting. Their conclusion, not to my astonishment, was that this claim should be met in full, albeit in stages. One amusing aspect, instructive to those who might be tempted to underestimate the ruthless cynicism of the Whitehall machine, was the decision by these officials that the Cabinet paper to Ministers reporting these recommendations for huge pay increases for themselves should make no mention of the astronomic total cost in public expenditure terms of around £1 billion. It was also decided not to mention the precise huge percentage pay increases involved for particular civil service grades. As one official said in my presence, 'Mention of such numbers might prejudice the ministerial discussion.' The civil servants also decided (not in my presence) that these particular papers concerning their own pay claims, alone among Cabinet papers on pay policy, should not be circulated to my Downing Street Policy Unit or to other special advisers. It was apparently felt that our comments (although we too as temporary civil servants benefited from this claim) would not be helpful and presumably might 'prejudice' Ministers. This was an excellent example of the benefits of what is known to political scientists as 'access' to government. (Other examples are the 1974 Cabinet decision to devolve parts of the civil service to the regions and the 1976 Cabinet decision to cut public expenditure on the civil service, the latter of which was only partly implemented and the former totally ignored by the bureaucracy supposed to impose these measures on itself.) That privilege of access was duly rewarded when, despite protests from the Policy Unit and courageously independent criticism from the individual civil servants in Downing Street, Ministers approved these vast although unspecified increases. Ministers considered that it was tough enough fighting workers outside and they certainly did not want to take on those in their own offices.

The school teachers, never slow to learn, promptly began to prepare strike action to back their own 36 per cent claim, although with less certainty of success because they did not have direct access to Cabinet. More daunting was the fact that ahead of us lay the massed ranks of the miners and the electricity supply workers. If we capitulated to filing clerks, what prospects did we have of fighting battalions with real clout?

With its anti-inflation policy in continuing disarray, the Government suffered a final blow at the beginning of March 1979 on the devolution referendum, when less than the statutory minimum of 40 per cent voted for constitutional change in Scotland. This defeat on one of Labour's major policy commitments – and moreover one on which repeated opinion polls had previously shown a Scottish majority – reflected not so much a change of mind on the matter of devolution as a decline in the reputation of the Labour Government. It also finally torpedoed the Prime Minister's parliamentary authority as he faced the inevitable vote of confidence and it lost the lobby support of the Scottish Nationalist MPs, which had been given only on the basis that Labour would bring in devolution, which could not now happen. The Liberals had, of course, already been detached since the end of the Lib-Lab pact in the previous summer and it now became clear that they would vote against the Government on any vote of confidence. Their leaders, David Steel and John Pardoe, old personal friends of mine, came home to dinner at this time to discuss the political outlook. They said that the Liberals wanted an early general election before the EEC elections in June because the Liberal party would then lose disastrously and they could not afford to suffer that blow to morale just ahead of a general election. They also believed that the Jeremy Thorpe scandal would come to court in July and would inevitably damage the Liberals. So the loose parliamentary coalition on which Labour depended was falling apart. Only the ill-matched partners from Ulster remained nominally in support of Mr Callaghan, although once the legislation giving the Unionists extra seats had been passed there was nothing in principle, in history or in personal affinity to bind them any longer. Henceforward the Government just drifted towards disaster.

It was a curious experience to be in a Government that knows that it will inevitably be defeated before long. It was like being on the sinking *Titanic*, although without the music. Neither Ministers nor civil servants did anything. No policy papers were circulated and there was no serious attempt to follow up the recent new agreement with the TUC. The only thing that did take place, regrettably, was the setting up of the Standing Commission on public sector pay comparability under the distinguished Chairmanship of one of its authors, Hugh Clegg. This had reverberations later because it was a major inflationary factor in 1979–81. Unfortunately no proper attempt was made to incorporate our suggested strict criteria of comparability which are necessary to ensure that such an exercise is not simply a bonanza for the public sector. Such a mechanism operating rigorously can resolve the pay problems which inevitably arise in public services not subject to market forces; indeed, it could beneficially be resorted to again by a future British government providing it is done with strict controls. However, comparability of pay without comparability of risk or effort is a bad principle for setting rewards in an economy. It is ironical that of all the ideas relating to pay pursued by Labour in the winter of 1978–9 that was the only one which survived, if only briefly.

During the March days following the devolution defeat the Prime Minister seemed depressed and inactive. He was clearly unhappy with this situation of drift and he told the Cabinet Economic Committee that he was fed up with living just from day to day. For some time it had seemed his objective to struggle through to a summer or autumn election in the hope that the situation might look better to the electorate later. Mr Callaghan now told his colleagues that he did not think it was right for a government to behave in this way; furthermore it was personally unacceptable to him. He proposed that, even if the Government won the imminent vote of confidence, we should anyway face the country at an early election in May.

The vote of confidence (which was actually a vote of censure by the Scottish Nationalists rather than a vote of no confidence by Mrs Thatcher) took place on Wednesday 28 March. The Prime Minister instructed his lieutenants that there was to be no wheeler-dealing beforehand to win lobby votes, and he specifically ordered Roy Mason not to try to buy off the Ulster Unionists (who by now had their legislation giving more Commons seats to Northern Ireland). In addition to losing the Unionists as well as the Liberals and the Scottish Nationalists, two Labour MPs had recently died leaving their seats vacant, so the numbers did not look good to begin with. Over the final days there were regular reports from the Whips to Downing Street on the state of play for Wednesday's vote. On the Monday and Tuesday the Whips thought that the Government was certain to lose, although hopefully only by two or three votes. Actually, the situation became more promising as support began to grow. It is easy now to forget that at that time there were many people who did not relish the prospect of a Thatcher administration and some politicians from the minor parties were looking for reasons not to bring down the Labour Government. On Wednesday our hopes were raised and the Whips reported that on the latest count we would survive: the result would be a draw and the Speaker would then by convention cast his vote for the Government. By the afternoon, however, our hopes were quickly evaporating. One Labour MP was seriously ill but we understood that he was going to be transported in a special ambulance to the precincts of the House to vote by being 'nodded through'. Whether through uncharacteristic compassion or customary incompetence, the party organisation failed to organise the ambulance in time and his vote was lost. (He died eleven days later.) Then at the last moment the Irish rebelled; Gerry Fitt voted against the Government and Frank Maguire abstained. Maguire, a Republican publican, disappointed but did not surprise us. Unpredictable at the best of times, he tended to vote with the party that had bought him his last drink. He was clearly under heavy pressure from political forces which in the end he dared not refuse. Certainly it was unusual for him to cross the Irish Sea simply to abstain. Gerry Fitt, a courageous and genuine Catholic Labour man, had delivered a much greater blow. Although he had a whole breadth of personal and political reasons for voting against the Government, his 'no' vote was probably the price we paid for our reactionary Irish policy. In the end we lost by one vote.

Immediately after the Commons defeat, the Conservative opposition was in touch with the Private Office in No. 10 asking to open contact with the civil service before the election. Certain conventions allow this and soon Mrs Thatcher and six of her senior colleagues were holding consultations with senior Whitehall officials, including the Cabinet Secretary and the Permanent Secretary at the Treasury, to discuss the changes which they would wish to make in various departmental policies and organisations. Thus, the Whitehall machine was preparing for change and the transition of power was starting to take place long before the Government was gone, or indeed before the election campaign had seriously begun.

The election campaign was to be unusually long by twentieth-century standards, covering six weeks including the Easter holiday. The general view of most academic and unbiased observers was that Labour actually won the campaign after starting 13 per cent behind in the polls, an unprecedented opening deficit for a sitting government. The gap closed marginally to an average of 12 per cent in the second week and 9 per cent in the third week. At one point after that it closed to 2 per cent but then the Tory lead widened out again. In the last few days before the election it fluctuated from 7 to 6 to 3 to 2·5 to 4 per cent. However, whatever the movements in the opinion polls (including one Tory lead of 21 per cent), the brutal fact was that Labour was always behind in every single national poll, in the polls of marginal seats and in polls on policy preferences.

Naturally the staff in Downing Street briefed the Prime Minister with as much election ammunition as possible, and that included attempts to boost morale with reminders that Labour had won the February 1974 election without ever leading in a single opinion poll. For a time the Prime Minister followed my proposal that he should in his speeches and on television repeatedly ask certain sharp questions relating to future Conservative policies on unemployment, prices, pensions and cuts in public services. Every day in No. 10 the Prime Minister's inner team had breakfast with him over which we discussed tactics and the contents of speeches and press releases. Organisationally Mr Callaghan's campaign outside London was conducted much better than in 1974, with Derek Gladwin, a senior trade unionist, and the Prime Minister's son, Michael, bringing a welcome professional touch. None the less, the political dimension was unsatisfactory. There was nobody to play Joe Haines's earlier role in writing hard-hitting speeches; there was actually no centralised and systematic discussion of the strategy and tactics of the campaign. Perhaps this was because it did not ever look to us as if we could win, however optimistic we may have been in our briefs to the Prime Minister. Whatever the electorate's reservations about Mrs Thatcher, they clearly preferred this devil they did not know to the devils of the Winter of Discontent whom they now knew only too well.

At 3.00 pm on polling day, 3 May 1979, before any count had begun, the Prime Minister telephoned from his Cardiff constituency to his Principal Private Secretary, Kenneth Stowe, to say that he was in no doubt that Mrs Thatcher would take over as Prime Minister the following day, Friday 4 May, and that his personal team should prepare to leave No. 10 by 3.30 in the afternoon. In the event the ninth Labour Government was pushed out by a swing of 7 per cent to the Conservatives.

Looking back on those five exhausting years of the 1974–9 Labour Governments, one main and inescapable conclusion is that the final failure was an internal defeat. The Conservative opposition never inflicted any serious damage on the Government during 1974–9. Although Labour was in a parliamentary minority throughout most of the time, nobody in No. 10 ever worried about the attacks from the Conservative party opposite. Mr Callaghan certainly always dominated Mrs Thatcher in the Commons, even at the end when he fatalistically seemed to accept imminent defeat. The occasional setbacks in the parliamentary lobbies – on private sector pay sanctions, or on the final vote of censure – were due to a few eccentric defections that had little to do with the central economic issues under debate. Significantly, even at the end, the Government was not defeated on a motion from the official Conservative opposition but one from the eccentric Scottish Nationalists, who behaved like turkeys voting for an early Christmas dinner.

Above all, although many factors contributed to its defeat, the Labour Government was finally undermined by the behaviour of certain of the trade unions and especially by the public sector unions during the Winter of Discontent. There is no question (setting aside for the moment the important longer-term trends that undoubtedly were also at work) that the public sector unions elected Mrs Thatcher in 1979; indeed, she subsequently said thank you to them in her own individual way. No one should have been in the least doubt as to what Mrs Thatcher would do to the public sector if elected. She is a commendably open and direct politician and she had always been quite clear about her intentions to cut public expenditure, to cut back public sector employment and to hold back public service pay. The public services employees – or at least the most active and vociferous groups among them – were organised by their local union activists to do everything possible to put Mrs Thatcher in a position of power where she could do just that. It was such short-sighted and irrational behaviour on their part that it requires analysis and explanation beyond the skills of the ordinary historian or political scientist, perhaps calling upon the less familiar social sciences of political and social psychology. There are times, as during the student riots of 1968, when irrational behaviour erupts in society and the fact that it is irrational does not mean that there are not real causes or that the established forces of government are not at fault. Most of the Labour Government's difficulties were of its own making and certainly much of the advice which it received from people such as myself was imperfect. Possibly the strict discipline of three years of rigid pay constraint, which allowed no flexibility or reflection of the particular needs or virtues or efforts of individual groups or persons, produced an inevitable counter-reaction. The activities of left-wing trade unionists who believed in total planning for the rest of society while insisting on an open-market free-for-all in respect of their own wage settlements also played an important part.

However, the anarchy which erupted was certainly nothing to do with the alleged relative bad circumstances of the public sector. Indeed, the public sector had never enjoyed such *relative* privilege as during 1974–9 when government expenditure on that sector as a percentage of national wealth was at its highest ever in peacetime. There was unprecedented redistribution of national resources towards the public service sector and public sector pay rose relative to the private sector as never before, so much so that when plans were made in early 1979 to establish a public sector pay comparability unit, an official paper from the Central Statistical Office pointed out that if the comparisons with the private sector were carried out rigorously there was a danger of there being widespread cuts in public sector pay. Public expenditure as a whole rose 9 per cent between 1974 and 1979, whereas the GDP was only 2·5 per cent higher. The public sector thus received a much bigger share of the national cake. Within these general figures was a redistribution of resources in line with Labour's announced priorities. Expenditure on defence was reduced by 10 per cent, while there was increased provision on housing of 56 per cent, on social security of 25 per cent and on support for industry of 75 per cent. Unemployment, which rose inevitably as the Western world slipped into the post-oil-shock recession, was deliberately kept out of the public sector and left to be inflicted almost wholly on private industry. No other British government (except perhaps Mr Wilson's 1964–70 administration) had treated the public sector with so much consideration. Yet the public sector was clearly not happy and wreaked dreadful damage on the Labour politicians who had devoted their lives to support of the public services. It is little wonder that Ministers looked so bemused in the winter of 1979.

Mrs Thatcher was also assisted towards victory by a number of other factors. The Labour Prime Minister's worries were all about holding together his own side. The Labour left wing's defeat of the private sector pay sanctions in November 1978 and the failure of the Scots to deliver their long-promised support for devolution in March 1979 each did their share of damage to the Government's authority in major policy areas. We lost the final decisive confidence vote technically because of the unpredictability of the Irish and failure to organise an ambulance for a sick MP. None of these eventualities was the consequence of Conservative action. In a series of self-inflicted wounds for the Labour movement, each of which might have been avoided, the party progressively undermined its own capacity to govern.

Both Mr Wilson and Mr Callaghan were highly experienced and supremely capable at the job of managing the Labour movement. In the changed structure of modern British politics it is possible that no party leader will again have their range of experience. Yet in the end it might be said that they failed. The Labour Government fell from power, deeply at odds with the trade union movement. The Labour party soon split apart as some 'moderates' formed a new party where they hoped not to have to live in daily conflict with the sectarian dogmatists of the left. Mr Callaghan looked in particular difficulty during 1978–9 because he was accustomed to working in comradeship with traditional trade union leaders. He had for a lifetime dealt on the basis that if he made a settlement with the top half a dozen union leaders he had made a deal which would stick. He made many such deals during 1978–9 but the union leaders were unable to deliver. In fact, the Labour Government and party, as well as its leader, failed fully to grasp that the union leaders could no longer guarantee to deliver their membership. The process of delegating power to local representatives – in which Jack Jones of the Transport and General Workers' Union was both an initiator and a victim when his union rejected his pleas on pay restraint in 1978 – had lately accelerated and gone too far for that. In addition, individual trade unionists no longer saw an automatic identity of interest with the political wing of the Labour movement. Mr Callaghan certainly understood that as well as anybody, and often discussed it, but there was little that he could do about it in 1979 when for the first time over half of all trade unionists failed to vote for the Labour party.

Of course, the problems were not all political. The unhelpful economic background, afflicting the whole Western world and not just Britain, was certainly a major problem which the Labour Governments of Mr Wilson and Mr Callaghan never overcame (in common with their fellow leaders, Schmidt, Giscard and Carter in Europe and the United States). In 1974 they inherited a quadrupled oil price, leading to a devastating combination of inflation and recession, and although they suffered the penalty of high oil prices they did not yet enjoy the revenue benefits which later flowed to Mrs Thatcher when the North Sea wells came on stream. Economic growth in the second half of the 1970s was inescapably at its lowest post-war level, in Britain as elsewhere in the industrial world. Without the necessary growth there were insufficient extra resources to satisfy the ever-expanding ambitions of the public and the personal sectors. The Labour Governments of 1974–9 were repeatedly in the position where they could only meet commitments to one section of the community by taking away from another; thus increased public sector expenditure meant increased taxation on the private sector. It is much easier to win elections after several years of 3 per cent growth, when it has been possible to divide up the increment in national resources and give some goodies to everybody. However, Mr Wilson and Mr Callaghan were never in that happy position. They redistributed away from a resentful private sector to an ungrateful public sector. This unavoidable lack of resources is not presented as an excuse but as a harsh fact of political life in the 1970s which is usually ignored by those left-wing critics who blamed the Labour Governments of this period for not delivering the moon, immediately. Perhaps the lesson is not to promise the moon.

A further general cause of defeat in 1979 was undoubtedly the extent to which the Labour Party had drifted apart from the electorate, including many of its own traditional working-class supporters. Some of the symptoms of the internal disease which later led to strife and electoral disaster in opposition in the early 1980s were already apparent during the earlier years in government. The party organisation was increasingly controlled by the far left and so the pressure from within the party, from conference, from the NEC and the constituency parties, was to make concessions to the left. Yet all tests of public opinion showed that the electorate was moving towards the right. Labour was becoming a party of minority principles and prejudices. This might not matter in a totalitarian state where the government is not accountable to the public, but in a democracy it is a bad basis for seeking an electoral majority. It placed Mr Callaghan in the uncomfortable, and ultimately untenable, dilemma of having to choose between pleasing his party or the public and it must be said that he managed this situation with remarkable skill until the gap between the party's priorities and the public's preference grew too wide.

My final reflection on Labour's defeat concerns the slow but irresistible tide of public opinion. Towards the end of the 1979 campaign I was travelling in the official Rover car with the Prime Minister. As we drove round Parliament Square towards Whitehall and Downing Street, I drew Mr Callaghan's attention to the recent improvement in the opinion polls, remarking that, with a little luck, and a few policy initiatives here and there, we might just squeak through. He turned to me and said quietly: 'I should not be too sure. You know there are times, perhaps once every thirty years, when there is a sea-change in politics. It then does not matter what you say or what you do. There is a shift in what the public wants and what it approves of. I suspect there is now such a sea-change – and it is for Mrs Thatcher.'

On the wider question of whether in Britain Cabinet government has given way to prime ministerial government, it must be said that Cabinet government was certainly alive and kicking in the 1970s, and it would be foolishly premature to assume that it has been killed off since. As long as there are Ministers with governmental experience and with personal political bases, especially if they are briefed by expert policy advisers, and as long as there are Prime Ministers (as there almost certainly will be again) who believe in the principle of Cabinet government and see the potential political advantages of spreading collective responsibility among colleagues and rivals, British government will remain based upon the Cabinet system.

Prime Ministers will, of course, continue to intervene and often make a major impact. Such action does not conflict with Cabinet government, but it is an intrinsic part of it – and if conducted properly is actually a strengthening factor. This book has illustrated how Mr Wilson and Mr Callaghan managed to do this successfully. Much evidence suggests that Mrs Thatcher has intervened more often and more dramatically. In the light of this it must be conceded that at times the British people have effectively a 'prime ministerial' form of government within the continuing and evolving Cabinet system. However, the strength of that prime ministerial dimension depends upon and varies with the inclinations, the temperament, the advisory support system and the current political prestige of the Prime Minister of the day. It also depends upon him or her being Chairman of the Cabinet within a Cabinet system. It does not mean that in Britain we yet have what could be meaningfully described as 'presidential' government. Cabinets have periods of subservience to dominant leaders. But over time, for as long as we retain parliamentary democracy, the British Cabinet system will probably survive the worst efforts of even the most strong-minded Prime Minister.

Index

193